Discipleship Junction

Where IS GOD?

Sheila Seifert and Beth Naylor

NEXGEN®

Building the New Generation of Believers

COOK COMMUNICATIONS MINISTRIES
Colorado Springs, Colorado • Paris, Ontario
KINGSWAY COMMUNICATIONS LTD
Eastbourne, England

NexGen® is an imprint of
Cook Communications Ministries
Colorado Springs, CO 80918
Cook Communications, Paris, Ontario
Kingsway Communications, Eastbourne, England

WHERE IS GOD?
© 2007 by Cook Communications Ministries

Cover Design: BMB Design
Cover Illustration: BMB Design/Ryan Putnam
Interior Design: TrueBlue Design/Sandy Flewelling
Interior Illustrations: Aline Heiser

First Printing 2007
Printed in the United States

1 2 3 4 5 6 7 8 9 10 Printing/Year 11 10 09 08 07

ISBN 978-0-7814-4444-6   104957

Table of Contents

WELCOME TO DISCIPLESHIP JUNCTION!

Discipleship Junction is an all-new program that harnesses the power of FUN to build young disciples through interaction with Bible truth and with each other.

A complete, multi-age children's ministry program, *Discipleship Junction* is packed full of interactive stories and drama, Scripture memory, and themed snacks and activities that will engage every child! It is guaranteed effective because its principles and methods of instruction are *teacher-tested* and *kid-approved*!

Intensive student-teacher interaction within a learning community that is relational and supportive makes *Discipleship Junction* an ideal program for including children with disabilities. Hands-on learning activities are easily adapted to include all students. For more ideas about inclusion, an excellent resource is *Let All the Children Come to Me* by MaLesa Breeding Ed.D., Dana Hood, Ph.D., and Jerry Whitworth, Ed.D., (Colorado Springs: Cook Communication Ministries, 2006).

Putting the Pieces Together

Get Set. We know you're busy, so we provide a list of materials and what you'll need to prepare for your lesson. You'll also need a photocopy machine and some basic classroom supplies: paper, pencils, markers, butcher paper, scissors, glue, and index cards. When you see this icon ⊗ allow a little extra prep time.

Kids love to dress up! Many of our Bible lessons use costume props from the *Bible time dress-up box*. This can be as simple as a box of items you gather from around the house or purchase inexpensively from a second-hand store. It should include: fake beards, an assortment of headcloths and robes or tunics, modern-day men's and women's clothes, props for worship dancers, and pretend microphones.

Tickets Please! *(10 minutes)* Each week begins with an activity option to involve children while others are being dropped off by parents.

■ The *Welcome Time Activity* will excite children's interest and help them connect with the Bible Truth for the week.

■ *Sweet treats.* Children are rewarded for attendance with a treat. God is pleased when children come and talk to Him. When they do, He rewards them with His presence. The treats remind us of that reward. Just fill a jar with individually wrapped treats (small candies, fruit snacks, etc.). Avoid foods typically associated with allergies. If you have diabetic students, remember to include sugar-free candies.

All Aboard for Bible Truth! *(20 minutes)* Whole group, interactive Bible lessons invite students ages 6–11 to participate in the entire lesson. Whether it's role-playing the story of the Samaritan or building trees out of cereal boxes, kids will be engaged in exciting, hands-on lessons.

■ Pre- and post-lesson discussion times encourage children to talk about their own life experiences and tie their knowledge to the week's Bible Truth.

■ *Use the Clues!* Practice is an important part of learning. *Where Is God?* uses the exciting theme of a treasure hunt—complete with a treasure map and clues—to help children practice and apply what they learn. Every week one significant clue from the lesson is added to the treasure map. In the weeks that follow, students are repeatedly challenged to remember the Bible Truth connected with each clue. These "memory hooks" help the Bible Truth stick with kids for a long time to come.

Bible Memory Waypoint (5 minutes). Toe tappin' and finger snappin' . . . there's nothing like the power of FUN to motivate children. Movement, rhythm, and role-play make it easy for kids to hide God's Word in their hearts (Psalm 119:11).

Prayer Station (15 minutes). Small group prayer time for children. Wow! What an idea! Children break into small groups of three to five with an adult helper—we call them StationMasters. Using reproducible instruction cards, adults guide children to share concerns, praise God, and practice the four activities of prayer: *praise, ask, confess, give thanks.*

(Optional) **Snack Stop and Activities** (10 minutes). Tied to the theme of the lesson, you have options for snacks and activities in which lesson truths are practiced and shared. Look for the throttle icon which shows the level of mess, energy, or noise required for the activity!

On the Fast Track! Reproducible take-home pages invite families to interact in and through fun activities and Bible memory.

Are you looking for an additional way to motivate young learners? *Discipleship Junction* includes an optional incentive program which rewards students for completing home activities. Children return a signed *Fast Track!* ticket and choose a prize from the treasure box. If you have a new student, you might welcome that child with the choice of a treasure, too! Simply cover and decorate a large shoebox. Fill with inexpensive items such as you might find at a party store.

HOW TO GET STARTED

1. **Begin by recruiting StationMasters**—adult helpers who will guide children through the process of praying in small groups. Each week you'll give the StationMasters a reproducible instruction card with the day's prayer theme and prayer suggestions to use with children in a small group. Don't have enough adult volunteers? How about recruiting middle- or high-schoolers to shepherd a group?

2. **Set up your room.** You'll need a big area for your large-group Bible teaching time. You'll also need to identify spaces for each of your small prayer groups. Don't forget that rearranging chairs and tables, or moving groups to a hallway is always an option. And children are willing helpers!

3. **Photocopy reproducibles** (see Resources) to parents and children's ministry helpers. Mail these two or three weeks before you begin your children's ministry program. Also copy *On the Fast Track!* pages for each child, and *StationMaster Cards* for each adult helper.

4. **Make a treasure map.** Tape together pieces of butcher paper to make a map measuring about 5' wide x 3' high. Then hand-copy the sample map (see Resources, 91) onto your paper with permanent marker. Crumple it and smooth it out again to add some drama. Don't worry if your map isn't identical to the sample! Hang the map at the front of your teaching area.

5. **Treasure map clues.** Copy the 13 clues (see Resources, 84-89), cut them out, and add some color. Lightly tape them to a poster board and display these on the wall next to your treasure map. Each week during *Use the Clues!* time, kids will find the right clue for that week's Bible truth and move it to the map where *X marks the spot.*

6. **Prepare student maps.** During the first lesson, children will have a chance to make a treasure map of their own to take home and track their journey toward the treasure. They'll find map clues identical to yours to make on their take-home papers each week. Don't forget to make a few extra maps for new students who may join the class later.

7. Gather and prepare your materials, set out your snacks, and you are ready to roll. So...
   FULL SPEED AHEAD! ALL ABOARD FOR DISCIPLESHIP JUNCTION!

LESSON ONE: Searching for God

Memory Verse:
You will seek me and find me when you seek me with all your heart (Jeremiah 29:13).

Bible Basis:
Jeremiah 29:13

Bible Truth:
When we search for God, we will find Him.

You Will Need:

- ☐ treasure map mounted on a wall
- ☐ old magazines
- ☐ bed sheet
- ☐ 10–15 accessories for the teacher to wear (i.e., belt, pin, ring, hat, glasses, etc.)
- ☐ 2 poster boards (28"x 22" each)
- ☐ 1 colored poster board (22"x14")
- ☐ treat jar
- ☐ *Use the Clues!* poster holding all 12 treasure map clues
- ☐ *On the Fast Track! #1* take-home paper
- ☐ *StationMaster Card #1*
- ☐ *(Optional)* treasure box
- ☐ *(Optional)* Snack: alphabet cereal, napkins
- ☐ *(Optional)* Activity #1: butcher paper, rubber bands
- ☐ *(Optional)* Activity #2: objects to hide such as small blocks, small treats, etc.

When you see this icon, it means preparation will take more than five minutes.

GET SET!
(Lesson Preparation)

- ■ Tape the Treasure Map to the wall where it will remain all quarter.
- ■ 🕐 Print Jeremiah 29:13 on the small, colored poster board so the words use the entire board: **You will seek me and find me when you seek me with all your heart (Jeremiah 29:13).** Make a frame from the larger poster board by centering the small board on it and tracing the outer edge. Cut the printed board into four jigsaw puzzle pieces. Assemble the jigsaw pieces again within the frame and trace each puzzle piece. Then, hide the jigsaw pieces around the room. Hang the frame in the classroom.
- ■ Cut butcher paper into about 4½' lengths for each child.
- ■ Make a copy of *On the Fast Track #1* for each child.
- ■ Make a copy of *StationMaster Card #1* for each helper.
- ■ Set out the treat jar and *(Optional)* treasure box.
- ■ Set up snack or outside play activities if you include these items in your Children's Ministry.
- ■ Print out discussion questions on separate pieces of paper.

TICKETS PLEASE!
(Welcome and Bible Connection)

- ■ *Objective: To excite children's interest and connect their own experiences with the Bible Truth, children will search magazines for treasure map features and discuss the meaning of the word "search."*
When everyone has arrived, call children to the lesson area and welcome them by name. Introduce new children to the group.

Welcome Time Activity: Geo Search

■ *Materials: old travel or geography magazines, scissors, glue sticks, poster board*
As children arrive, let them examine the treasure map. Have helpers invite children to search through magazines to find and cut out examples of geographic features on the map: mountains, swamps, geysers, bogs, etc. As they search, helpers can engage children in conversation. **What does it mean to search? What have you had to search for before? Have you seen the places shown on the treasure map?** Let them glue the pictures they find collage-style on a piece of poster board.

Offer each child a treat from the treat jar. Say: **God is pleased when children search for Him. When they do, He rewards them with His presence. The treats remind us of that reward.** Children may finish their treat now, or save it.

Sharing Time and Bible Connection

Introduce today's lesson by putting on 10–15 accessories as you talk. Then drape a sheet over yourself to hide the accessories. Have a helper hand out papers and pencils. Ask students to list as many accessories as they remember. Helpers can help younger children with writing. After a minute or two, take off the sheet and see who remembered the most items.

After the object lesson, help your students connect their ideas to the Bible story they're about to hear from Jeremiah 29:13. **You saw me put on each accessory, but no one remembered every thing I had on. Sometimes we see things, but forget about them until we take another look. That's true about God, too! We can forget that God is there until we take a closer look. <u>But when we search for God, we will find Him</u>.**

 ## ALL ABOARD FOR BIBLE TRUTH   Jeremiah 29:13
(Bible Discover and Learn Time)

■ *Objective: Children will study Jeremiah 29:13 to learn that if they search for God, they will find Him.*
■ *Materials: Use the Clues! poster with map clues.*

How many of you have been on a treasure hunt? What treasures did you find? Allow several children to share what they found. **Is the treasure you found in that hunt as special to you today as it was when you found it? Just what is a treasure anyway?** Let children suggest definitions and examples.
Think of the things that are really important to you. Which thing is most

important to you? Let volunteers share their ideas. Share one of your own if you choose.

People have different ideas about what a treasure is. Some people spend a lot of time searching for a treasure they think is valuable. We're going to make small groups and talk about different kinds of things people search for, then each group will share what they talked about.

Divide kids into four to six multi-age groups and assign a helper to each. Give each group a discussion question and instruct them to choose a "speaker" who will explain their answer to the class. (More than one group may discuss each question depending on how many small groups you create.)

Discussion questions:

1. How long would you search for a comb or brush? Do you have more than one at home? If you had other ones, how hard would you hunt for a lost one?
2. How long would you look for a book or toy you really wanted? How long would that toy or book be very, very special to you?
3. How long and hard would you search to find the perfect friend or pet? How would you know when you found the best one?
4. How long would you search for a box full of money? What would you feel like if you searched for a long, long time and didn't find it?

Give groups three to five minutes for discussion, then call everyone back together. Group "speakers" will take turns sharing their group question and answer. Then, summarize: **There are so many things we search for. Some are things we think are really important today, but next week we don't feel the same way about them. Toys can break. Money gets lost. Friends might not want to be together any more. Sometimes, we hunt for some treasures and never find them, no matter how hard and how long we look.**

But there is one treasure that I know _for sure_ **you and I can find if we search for it. In fact, the Bible promises we'll find it. The promise is in Jeremiah 29:13.** Read the verse from your Bible. Then, write the verse on the board, but leave blank spaces for "you" and "your."

This is a totally true promise, and it means the most valuable treasure in the world is one we can find for sure.

Write a child's name in the two blanks of the verse, then read it, prefacing it with "God says." Read it again with another child's name. Ask children to turn to someone near them and say the verse to that person, using the person's name. Helpers should join up with anyone who doesn't find a partner.

There's one problem with searching for God. What do you think it might be? Let kids respond. **Yes, it's forgetting to search! We remember to search for the ball we left on the sidewalk, or for a school backpack. But since we can't see God the same way we see our toys or pets or homework, we forget to search for Him. If we forget to search for God, will we find Him?** Let kids shout no, ask the question again and let them shout louder. Do this a few times.

For these 13 weeks, we're going to be searching for God. A cool treasure map is our way of remembering about this search.

Use the Clues!
(Bible Review)

Okay, let's see what you remember.

- **What do we sometimes forget to search for?** (God)
- **What did God promise to those who seek Him?** (He promised He would be found)
- **How does God say we have to search?** (with all our hearts)
- **What should we do when we forget about God?** (search for Him again)

Explain how the treasure map will work this quarter: **We are going to use this map to help us search for treasure. Every week, we'll add a new clue to this map. Hey! How would you like to have your own map like this one?** Let kids respond. **Today we'll make a map you** can take home to hang in your bedroom or somewhere else in your house. Each week, on your *Fast Track!* papers there will be a clue for your map just like the one we use in class. You can color your clue and attach it to your treasure map at home. On the last week of class, everyone who brings their treasure maps back to show the rest of the class will get a great reward. If you miss a week or two, don't worry. You can mark your treasure map with as many clues as you have collected.

Go to the treasure map. **We start here.** Point to the start. **This week, we have to climb over the Mountains of Forgetfulness. How do we do that?** Hold up the clue and read it. **"When we search for God, we will find Him."** That's an important clue in our search for treasure.

BIBLE MEMORY WAYPOINT
(Scripture Memory)

Jeremiah 29:13

- ***Objective:*** *Children will hide God's Word in their hearts for guidance, protection, and encouragement.*

To search for God, we have to search God's holy Word, the Bible. This week the Bible verse is hidden in our classroom so you'll have to search for it.

Divide the class into four groups. Each group will search for one puzzle piece. As the pieces are found, use double-sided tape to attach them to the frame. **Let's see which group can find a piece and be the first to sit down and be silent.** When all the groups have finished, say the verse and reference together two to three times: **You will seek me**

and find me when you seek me with all your heart (Jeremiah 29:13).

Then have each group say only those words that were on their puzzle piece. You can have them stand when they talk and sit down when done, making it a more active and fun rehearsal. Repeat the activity a couple of times before you have the whole class say the Bible verse together again. Keep the poster board frame to use again during the quarter.

 ## PRAYER STATION

- **Objective:** *Children will explore and practice prayer for themselves.*
- **Materials:** *Copies of* StationMaster Card #1 *for each helper*

Break into small groups of three to five children. Assign a teen or adult helper to each small group and give each helper a copy of StationMaster Card #1 (see Resources, 93).

 ## SNACK STOP: GOD SPELL (Optional)

If you plan to provide a snack, this is an ideal time to serve it.

- **Materials:** *alphabet cereal, napkins*

Pour a small pile of cereal on each child's napkin. Have them search for the letters in the word, "God." Challenge them to create as many spellings of "God" as they can before eating the cereal. For younger children, print "God," on the board.

Note: Always be aware of children with food allergies and have another option on hand if necessary.

 ## APPLICATION

- **Objective:** *Children will have opportunities to show how the lesson works in their own lives through activities and take-home papers.*

Some children's ministries may allow children to play outside at this point. If yours does not, choose one of the following activities.

Take-Home Treasure Maps

■ **Materials:** *butcher paper sections, markers, rubber bands*

Give children as much time as possible to make a version of the treasure map to use at home. Provide art supplies and a section of butcher paper for each child. Let them spread out on the tables and floor to work. They'll use your class map as the example. Ask older children and helpers to assist younger children. Have kids roll up and rubber band their map to take home, with instructions to parents about mounting the map and its home use.

Hide and Seek

■ **Materials:** *small objects to hide*

Build up the excitement for this quarter's theme of searching for God by having a treasure hunt. Choose something you will hide; hide the objects—some hard places, some easy—around the room. Divide into two or more teams. Let children search for the objects. When they've all been found, have them tell you how they felt searching and finding the objects. Connect those feelings of excitement, satisfaction, and thrill to searching for and finding God.

ON THE FAST TRACK! *(Take-Home Papers)*

(Optional) Introduce the treasure box: **Who would like to choose a prize from the treasure box?** Expect excited responses. **Today I'm going to give each of you an** *On the Fast Track!* **paper to take home. When you've done the activities and memorized the Bible verse, ask a parent to sign the ticket** (show ticket). **When you bring that back next week, you'll get to have a turn at the treasure box.**

Distribute the take-home papers and each child's treasure map just before the children leave.

LESSON TWO: All in the Family

Quicksand of Unthankfulness

Memory Verse:
Give thanks in all circumstances, for this is God's will for you in Christ Jesus (1 Thessalonians 5:18).

Bible Truth:
We find God through the people in our families.

Bible Basis:
Exodus 20:12; Leviticus 19:3; Deuteronomy 1:31; Proverbs 1:8, 13:1, 15:5, 22:6; Isaiah 66:13; Mark 10:16; Ephesians 6:1-4; Colossians 3:20; 1 Thessalonians 2:7; Hebrews 12:7

You Will Need:

- [ ] treasure map mounted on a wall
- [ ] 4 poster boards
- [ ] 3 towels or dishcloths large enough to cover poster boards
- [ ] pretend microphone (paper towel tube, paper cup, etc.)
- [ ] treat jar
- [ ] *Use the Clues!* poster with map clues
- [ ] *On the Fast Track! #2* take-home paper
- [ ] *StationMaster Card #2*
- [ ] *(Optional)* treasure box
- [ ] *(Optional)* Snack: plain cookies, icing, sprinkles, plastic spoons
- [ ] *(Optional)* Activity #1: craft sticks, paper, brown, yellow and black yarn
- [ ] *(Optional)* Activity #2: dress up box (with shirts, pants, dresses or skirts, jewelry, shoes, etc.)

When you see this icon, it means preparation will take more than five minutes.

 GET SET!
(Lesson Preparation)

- ■ On one poster board, draw a dad (or cut from a magazine). On another board, draw a mom (or cut from a magazine). On the third board, draw a child (or cut from a magazine). Prop each on a chair and drape with a towel.
- ■ Print today's bible memory verse on a poster board: **Give thanks in all circumstances, for this is God's will for you in Christ Jesus (1 Thessalonians 5:18).**
- ■ Hang the poster board on the wall at the front of the classroom.
- ■ Make a copy of *On the Fast Track #2* take-home paper for each child.
- ■ Make a copy of *StationMaster Card #2* for each helper.
- ■ Set out the treat jar and *(optional)* treasure box.
- ■ Set up snack or outside play activities if you include these items in your children's ministry.
- ■ If using activity option #1, create stick puppets of your family. Draw a face on a 3" paper oval, and glue it to the top of a craft stick. Add yarn hair. Repeat for each member of your family.

TICKETS PLEASE!
(Welcome and Bible Connection)

■ **Objective:** *To excite children's interest and connect their own life experiences with the Bible Truth, children will play a game about family members.*

Welcome Time Activity: Family Member Search

■ **Materials:** *none*

Have your adult or teen helper explain the game: Players will search out others who have a family member with the named quality. For example, say: **Find someone who has a little brother.** Once kids find someone with the named quality, name a new quality. You might suggest: two grandmothers; a father with a name that starts with R; an aunt; an older brother; an older sister; more than two brothers or sisters; a mom with brown hair.

When everyone has arrived, call children to the lesson area and welcome them. Offer them a treat from the *treat jar*. Say: **God loves it when children search for Him. When they do, He rewards them with His presence. The treats remind us of that reward.** Children may finish their treat now or take it home.

Sharing Time and Bible Connection

Introduce today's lesson by discussing these questions. As you talk, give every child an opportunity to say something.

■ **What is the name for the group of people who live at home with us?** (our families)

■ **Raise your hand if you don't have any brothers or sisters. Do you have a family?** (yes)

■ **Jump to your feet if you do have brothers or sisters or both. Do you have a family?** (yes)

■ **Clap your hands once if you live with your grandparents, foster parents, cousins, or another relative. Do you have a family?** (yes)

After this sharing time, help your students connect their discussion to the Bible story they are about to hear. **God gave each of us a special and unique family! Today we'll discover from the Bible how <u>we find God through the people in our families.</u>**

ALL ABOARD FOR BIBLE TRUTH!
(Bible Discover and Learn Time)

■ *Objective: Children will study various passages to discover how they can find God in their own families.*
■ *Materials: pretend microphone, mother, father and child posters, three towels or cloths, Use the Clues! poster with map clues.*

Set each of the three family member posters on a chair and cover with a cloth. Talk like a game show announcer into a pretend microphone. **I have three special guests to introduce to you today.**

Let's meet Guest #1! Gesture to the covered dad picture. **According to Exodus 20:12, you are to honor this person. God says you must respect this person. This person carried you when you were young. You should listen to this person's instruction. This person disciplines you for your own good. This person can train and help you understand God. Who is this person?** Let children guess. Unveil the dad poster.

Our dads are really an important part of our lives. If you don't have a dad, think of someone in your life who sometimes acts like a father to you.

Let's meet Guest #2! You are also to honor this person. You are to obey this person. This person teaches you. Isaiah 66:13 says that this person comforts you. This person gently cares for you. Who is this person? Gesture toward the mom poster. Unveil the poster. **This person is a mother! Without a mother, you wouldn't learn many things you need to learn to grow up. Our moms are so important in our families. If you don't have a mom, think of someone in your life who sometimes acts like a mother to you.**

I have one more special guest to introduce. Let's meet Guest #3! This guest needs to be trained. Jesus said He especially loved this kind of person. This person needs to learn to obey parents. And this person is meant to grow up knowing and following God. Who is this person? Gesture to last poster. Unveil the poster. **It's you and kids like you! Whether you are the only child in your family or you have a dozen brothers and sisters, your family is special and unique.**

Now who decided just who would be in your family? (God) **Some families have children who were born from their moms, and some have children who were adopted into the family. It doesn't matter which way you got to your family, because God created your family the way He wanted it to be.**

Here is an important question: why did God make families anyway? (Let children offer suggestions.) **Yes, you're thinking in the right direction. Families show us a picture of what God is like.**

When your dad teaches you how to use a hammer or reads you a story, you can remember there is another strong Father who loves and teaches you. It's God in heaven! When your mom holds you close and listens when you've gotten hurt, God is showing you that He comforts

and cares for you, too. Remember the last time you had a fight with your brother or sister, and he or she forgave you for being mad? When family members forgive each other, it is a picture of how God forgives us when we act badly.

No one likes to be disciplined, do they? Yet, even when your parents correct you for disobeying them, that also teaches about God. God disciplines all of us because He loves us and wants us to obey Him. <u>In our families, we can see God</u>.

Ask children to share a time when someone in their family showed God's love. If you have a large class, divide into smaller groups for this brief sharing time. **Yes, these are all examples of how we can <u>find more of who God is through the people in our families</u>**. Point to the treasure map. **That's why we should look for God in them and be thankful for our families. That's what keeps us from getting stuck in the Quicksand of Unthankfulness.**

Direct kids' attention to the *Use the Clues!* poster where map clues are displayed. **Which clue did we discover today?** Help children decide that today's lesson was about the "God teaches us about Himself through families" clue. Ask a volunteer to take it off the board and attach it to the map.

Use the Clues!
(Bible Review)

Let's see what you remember from our lesson today.

- **What people does God use to show you about Himself?** (parents, siblings, grandparents, other family members)
- **How does God use your family to teach Him about Himself?** (the ways our parents teach us things, comfort us, discipline us, encourage us, the ways our brothers and sisters forgive us, show us love, help us—all these are ways we find what God is like)
- **When do you find God in your family?** (when people at home show patience, kindness, forgiveness, discipline, etc.)
- **What can we do now that we know we can find God in our families?** (be thankful for each person in our families)

At this point each week, trace the treasure map clues to help children review the Bible Truth and remember ways they can find God.

BIBLE MEMORY WAYPOINT   1 Thessalonians 5:18
(Scripture Memory)

- ***Objective:** Children will hide God's Word in their hearts for guidance, protection, and encouragement.*

Read this week's memory verse from the poster, pointing to each word:

Give thanks in all circumstances, for this is God's will for you in Christ Jesus (1 Thessalonians 5:18).

Teach the verse by doing an echo rap. Have the kids stand facing you. Use a cool tone of voice and say **Give.** The kids should repeat it the same way you said it. Do it again, adding a word: **Give thanks.** Then the kids repeat just like you said it. Keep adding one word and having children repeat each time. Vary your voice to add drama and challenge the children to imitate you. Invite a child to lead the next repetition.

PRAYER STATION

- **Objective:** *Children will explore and practice prayer for themselves in small groups.*
- **Materials:** *Copies of* StationMaster Card #2 *for each adult or teen helper*

Break the large group into small groups of three to five children. Assign a teen or adult helper to each small group and give each helper a copy of StationMaster Card #2 (see Resources, 94) with ideas for group discussion and prayer.

SNACK STOP: COOKIE FAMILIES (Optional)

If you plan to provide a snack, this is an ideal time to serve it.

- **Materials:** *plain cookies, icing, candy sprinkles, plastic spoons*

Hand out cookies to children. Give each child a spoonful of icing. Using icing and sharing the sprinkles, children can decorate their cookies to look like someone in their family.
    Note: Always be aware of children with food allergies and have another option on hand if necessary.

APPLICATION

- **Objective:** *Children will have opportunities to show how the lesson works in their own lives through activities and take-home papers.*

Some children's ministries may allow children to play outside at this point. If yours does not, choose one of the following activities.

Puppet Families

- **Materials:** *craft sticks, glue, markers, scissors, yarn*

Let's make a set of stick puppets that's just like each of our families. Show them your stick puppet family. Have helpers hand out supplies so each child can make a puppet for each family member at home. When done, let children each find a place in the classroom where their puppets can "live." They can then go over to each other's houses and visit or play. Encourage them to ask a question about something the other family does, such as, "Where does your family eat breakfast?" or "If your family plays dodge ball, show me how your family would play." Children will take their puppet family home as a reminder to thank God for showing Himself to them through the people in their family.

Family Life Relay

- **Materials:** *dress up box (with shirts, pants, dresses or skirts, jewelry, shoes, etc.)*

Divide into two or more teams, with at least four people per team. Set the dress up box at the far end of the playing area. Have teams line up at the opposite end of the area. Explain that the first player in the line is the father. Next is the mother; the others are children. At the starting signal, the first members of each team race to the box and put on two items that would be appropriate dad clothes. Each races back, then the next member on the team races to the box and puts on two pieces of mom clothes. The children put on any two things appropriate to kids. The first team to be all dressed and back in line wins. You can play again and have team members take off their dress-up gear this time.

ON THE FAST TRACK! *(Take-Home Papers)*

(Optional) Treasure box. Hand out the take-home papers, and explain how children can use *On the Fast Track!* papers to continue making their treasure maps and clues at home. **Today I'm going to give every child an *On the Fast Track!* paper to take home. There are activities to do and a Bible verse to memorize on each sheet. To earn a prize, complete all the activities this week and learn your verse. When you're finished, ask your parents or guardian to sign the ticket. Bring it with you next week and you'll get to choose a prize from the treasure box!**

Distribute the take-home papers just before children leave.

LESSON THREE: Among Friends

Memory Verse:
A friend loves at all times (Proverbs 17:17).

Bible Basis:
1 Samuel 13—20

Bible Truth:
We find God through our friendships.

Swamp of Unfriendliness

You Will Need:

- [ ] treasure map mounted on wall
- [ ] 1 poster board
- [ ] 4 balloons
- [ ] play dough
- [ ] treat jar
- [ ] *Use the Clues!* poster with map clues
- [ ] *On the Fast Track! #3* take-home paper
- [ ] *StationMaster Card #3*
- [ ] (Optional) treasure box
- [ ] (Optional) Snack: any snack that is comprised of two parts that go together very well, such as mini bagels and cream cheese, peanut butter and jelly (on crackers), cheese and crackers
- [ ] (Optional) Activity #1: paper, crayons, markers, or colored pencils

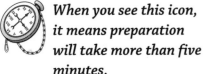 **When you see this icon, it means preparation will take more than five minutes.**

 ## GET SET!
(Lesson Preparation)

- ■ Print today's Bible memory verse on a poster board: **A friend loves at all times (Proverbs 17:17).**
- ■ Blow up and tie the balloons. On one draw an excited face, on the second a sad face, on the third a mad face, and on the last a scared face.
- ■ Make a copy of *On the Fast Track #3* take-home paper for each child.
- ■ Make a copy of *StationMaster Card #3* for each helper.
- ■ Set out the treat jar, and *(optional)* treasure box.
- ■ Set up snack or outside play activities if you include these items in your children's ministry.

TICKETS PLEASE!
(Welcome and Bible Connection)

- ■ *Objective: To excite children's interest and connect their own life experiences with the Bible Truth, children will mold friends out of play dough.*

Welcome Time Activity: Play Dough Friends

■ *Materials: play dough*

As children arrive, invite them to make themselves and one or more friends of play dough. Ask them to mold the play dough friends doing things the children like to do with friends, like playing soccer, going to the park or playing with dolls.

When everyone has arrived, call children to the lesson area and welcome them. Offer them a treat from the *treat jar*. Say: **God is really pleased when children search for Him. He rewards their searching by letting you find Him. Finding God is a sweet thing. These treats are a reminder that God wants us to search for Him.** Children may finish their treat now or take it home.

Sharing Time and Bible Connection

Introduce today's lesson by discussing these questions. As you talk, give every child an opportunity to say something.

■ *Materials: 4 inflated balloons, each with a facial expression (excited, sad, mad, scared)*

■ **If one of your good friends felt like this,** (show a balloon face), **what would you say or do for them?**

■ **If you felt this way** (show a different balloon face), **what would one of your good friends say or do for you?** Repeat these questions with the remaining two balloons.

After this sharing time, help your students connect their discussion to the Bible story they are about to hear from 1 Samuel 13—20:

When you feel excited or sad or angry or scared a good friend can listen to you, show they care, be excited with you, or help you work out your feelings. Friends are really an important part of life. Think how lonely and hard life would be with no one to cheer you up, share your great news, play and laugh. Good friends aren't just fun, <u>they help us find more about God.</u>

ALL ABOARD FOR BIBLE TRUTH

1 Samuel 13–20

(Bible Discover and Learn Time)

- **Objective:** *Children will study 1 Samuel 13—20 to find out how the friendship between David and Jonathan showed love.*
- **Materials:** *Use the Clues! poster with map clues*

Everyone is going to be part of the storytelling team today. Divide the class in half and have each half stand on the opposite side of the story area. Assign one group to be the Jonathan group; the other is the David group. Assign a helper to each group. If possible, have the helpers read the story text before class so they have ideas how to mime the story. They'll help the children act out the two friends as you narrate the passage.

1 Samuel has a terrific story about two young men who were best friends. They were named David and Jonathan. Jonathan was the son of King Saul. He fought many battles with his father. He was brave. Have the Jonathans hold up their arms and display their muscles to show they're strong. **David was a sheepherder who became a soldier and also fought many battles.** Have the Davids pretend to gather sheep, and then move as if they are fighting battles.

God told King Saul, that his son, Jonathan, would not be king after him. God wanted David to be the king instead. This should have made Jonathan angry at David. Have the Jonathans look angry. **But he wasn't mad at David. Jonathan felt like he and David were true friends.** Have the Jonathans and Davids shake hands.

They made a covenant, or promise, with each other. To show their promise, Jonathan gave David his robe, tunic, sword, bow, and belt. Have the Jonathans pretend to take off and give their robes and tunics, swords, bows, and belts to the Davids.

Jonathan showed his friendship to David in other ways. One time, he saved David's life when King Saul wanted to kill him. David also showed his friendship. He promised to never hurt Jonathan or his family. Have the Davids hold up pretend shields in front of the Jonathans.

A day came when David and Jonathan had to leave each other. They didn't know if they would ever see each other again, David bowed down to Jonathan three times, so that his face touched the ground. Have the Davids bow down three times. **In the Hebrew custom, they kissed each other and cried.** Pause, and then have the Davids and Jonathans pretend to cry.

David and Jonathan were best friends. Thank your volunteers for their help, and have them sit down.

How did Jonathan and David show their friendship? Have students give ideas; write them on the white board. When the list is done, ask the children to think about how friends care for each other just like God cares for us. (i.e., God is there for us, He protects us, He cares about our feelings, etc.).

God is all of these things! He's our very best friend. Whenever we hang out with our friends and enjoy each other, we can think about how

God wants to share in our lives just the same way. <u>We find God and what He's like through our true friends</u>.

Point to the treasure map. <u>We can find God's love for us through our friends</u>. We also need to BE a good friend so others will see God's love through us. If we do that, we will be able to trek through the Swamp of Unfriendliness. Which clue did we discover today? Help children decide that today's lesson was about the "We find God through our friendship" clue. Choose a child to take it off the *Use the Clues!* board and place it on the map.

Use the Clues!
(Bible Review)

Let's review our lesson with some questions.

- **What was David and Jonathan's friendship like?** (they were the best of friends, they cared about each other)
- **How did Jonathan show his friendship to David?** (he gave David his robe, tunic, sword, bow, and belt; he saved David's life when King Saul wanted to kill him)
- **How did David show his friendship to Jonathan?** (he promised to never hurt Jonathan or his family)

- **How do we find God because of our friends?** (we feel love and care from our friends, friends are faithful and loyal, we want the best for them)

Jonathan and David's friendship was very close. They loved each other and showed it. When we experience a true friend's love for us, we feel the love of God in a real way. And we can show the love of God by the way we are unselfish and loving toward our friends.

At this point each week, follow the *Use the Clues!* found in the *Resource* section to help children review the Bible Truth and remember ways they can search for God. Review all weeks up to this week.

BIBLE MEMORY WAYPOINT   Proverbs 17:17
(Scripture Memory)

- *Objective: Children will hide God's Word in their hearts for guidance, protection, and encouragement.*

Read this week's memory verse from the poster, pointing to each word:

A friend loves at all times (Proverbs 17:17).

To help children memorize the Bible verse, play "follow the leader." Say the verse a line at a time and have the class repeat it after you. Do this a few times until the verse is familiar. Then let volunteers take turns "leading" the class in a different way to say the verse. They might instruct the class to say it with both hands on their head, while hopping on one foot, or in their "opera" voice. Remind leaders that they need to make good choices as they lead.

PRAYER STATION

- ■ **Objective:** *Children will explore and practice prayer for themselves in small groups.*
- ■ **Materials:** *Copies of* StationMaster Card #3 *for each adult or teen helper*

Break into small groups of three to five children. Assign a teen or adult helper to each small group and give each helper a copy of *StationMaster Card #3* (see Resources, 94) with ideas for group discussion and prayer.

SNACK STOP: GO-TOGETHER GOODIES (Optional)

If you plan to provide a snack, this is an ideal time to serve it.

- ■ **Materials:** *any snack that is comprised of two parts that go together well, such as mini bagels and cream cheese, peanut butter and jelly (on crackers), cheese and crackers*

Set the two items on the tables. Ask children to find a partner. Each partner will take enough of one of the two items and share them with the other partner. Ask children to talk about a way they want to show care to a friend this week.

Note: Always be aware of children with food allergies and have another option on hand if necessary.

APPLICATION

■ *Objective: Children will have opportunities to show how the lesson works in their own lives through activities and take-home papers.*

Some children's ministries may allow children to play outside at this point. If yours does not, choose one of the following activities.

Friendship Cards

■ *Materials: paper, crayons, markers, or colored pencils*
Demonstrate how to fold the paper in half to make a greeting card. Explain that children will use this time to make a card for a friend. **Think about one friend who reminds you of God. Decorate the front of your card to show how this friend reminds you of God. On the inside, thank your friend for showing you who God is.** Helpers should move about the room to help write the inside of the cards for children who can't write yet. Ask each child how they'll give their card to the friend they made it for.

When Does a Friend Love? Game

Have children divide into mixed-age pairs or small groups of three. Each group will think of one difficult or problem situation a person can have, then how friends could show love to them "at all times" as the memory verse says. Pairs or groups plan a short drama to show the problem and how the "friends" demonstrate love. Those watching guess what the problem is and how the friends are displaying love.

ON THE FAST TRACK! *(Take-Home Papers)*

(Optional) Bring out the treasure box. **Who would like to choose a prize from the treasure box?** Show the *On the Fast Track!* take-home papers. **Today in your *On the Fast Track!* papers, there are activities to do and a Bible verse to memorize. To earn a prize, after you do the activities this week and learn your verse, ask your parents or guardian to sign the ticket and bring it next week!**
Distribute the take-home papers just before children leave.

Great Lonely Desert

Memory Verse:
God has said, "Never will I leave you; never will I forsake you" (Hebrews 13:5b).

Bible Truth:
We find God in our everyday lives.

Bible Basis:
Genesis 1:11–12, 24-25;
Psalms 4:8; 23:1–4; 34:4; 40:1;
46:1; 84:11; 85:12; 147:8;
1 Timothy 4:4; 2 Timothy 3:16

You Will Need:

- [ ] treasure map mounted on a wall
- [ ] 1 poster board
- [ ] small soft ball
- [ ] Send home note for "clean trash" for next week
- [ ] treat jar
- [ ] *Use the Clues!* poster with map clues
- [ ] *On the Fast Track! #4* take-home paper
- [ ] *StationMaster Card #4*
- [ ] *(Optional)* treasure box
- [ ] *(Optional)* Snack: pretzel sticks, trail mix, small bowls
- [ ] *(Optional)* Activity #2: Shrink plastic, baking trays, permanent markers, clear packing tape, scissors, safety pins

When you see this icon, it means preparation will take more than five minutes.

GET SET!
(Lesson Preparation)

- ■ 🕐 Print today's Bible memory verse on a poster board: **God has said, "Never will I leave you; never will I forsake you" (Hebrews 13:5b).** Hang the poster board on the wall at the front of the classroom.
- ■ 🕐 Write and photocopy a note to send home with students, asking families to send "clean trash" next week, such as all sorts of boxes, plastic containers, packing paper, etc.
- ■ Print out the list of Bible references on page 29. Cut the list apart so each reference is on a separate slip of paper: **Genesis 1:11–12; Genesis 1:24–25; Psalm 4:8; Psalm 23:1–4; Psalm 34:4; Psalm 40:1; Psalm 46:1; Psalm 84:11; Psalm 85:12; Psalm 147:8; 1 Timothy 4:4; 2 Timothy 3:16**
- ■ Make a copy of *On the Fast Track #4* take-home paper for each child.
- ■ Make a copy of *StationMaster Card #4* for each helper.
- ■ Set out the treat jar and *(optional)* treasure box.
- ■ Set up snack or outside play activities if you include these items in your children's ministry.

TICKETS PLEASE!
(Welcome and Bible Connection)

- ■ ***Objective:*** *To excite children's interest and connect their own life experiences with the Bible Truth, children will play a game of observation and talk about where God is in their everyday lives.*

Welcome Time Activity: I Spy

- *Materials:* *none*

   As children arrive, have helpers start them playing the game "I Spy" to make them aware of what's around them. Play in the room and even outside (or by looking out a window). One person chooses something he sees and gives a single clue about its shape, color, size or use. He uses this phrase to give his clues: I spy with my little eye something (pink/round/metal/etc.). Others intently search and try to guess the object. The one who guesses gets to choose the next object to be "spied."

When everyone has arrived, call children to the lesson area and welcome them. Offer them a treat from the treat jar. Say: **God likes it when you and I search for Him. Whenever we do, He rewards us with His presence. The treats remind us of that reward.** Children may eat their treat or take it home.

Sharing Time and Bible Connection

   Introduce today's lesson with a discussion. Begin by tossing a ball to a child and asking: **What is your favorite time of day?** After answering, ask the child why. After child answers, ask for the ball to be tossed back to you. Toss it to another child and ask the question again. Do this several times.

- **Where is God in our everyday lives?**
- **How do you think you can see God when you're doing a chore or playing with your friends or at school?**
- **Do you think there is some time of the day or night, or during the week when God isn't there? How do you know?** (no, the Bible tells us God never leaves us)

   We know we can find God in some places and situations, but we often forget to look for Him in everyday times. Most people never think of God being with them when they're brushing their teeth or waking up on a Saturday morning. Is He there? Today we're going to find out <u>where God is in our everyday lives</u>.

ALL ABOARD FOR BIBLE TRUTH
(Bible Discover and Learn Time)

- **Objective:** *Children will study Genesis 1:11–12; 1:24–25; Psalms 4:8; 23:1–4; 34:4; 40:1; 46:1; 84:11; 85:12; 147:8; 1 Timothy 4:4; and 2 Timothy 3:16 to understand how they can find God in their everyday lives.*
- **Materials:** *Use the Clues! poster with map clues, verse slips, extra Bibles, pencils*

Divide the class into small groups of two or more children, pairing younger children with older ones. The older child can find the reference and point to it as they read. Ask helpers to assist groups as they need it.

Hand out one verse to each group and be sure all children have Bibles. Each group will find their verse and decide what truth it tells them about God being in their everyday lives. Then they will search the room to find an object that represents that truth. After about 10 minutes, ask groups to come back together. Each group will read their verse in turn and describe how their object represents how God is part of their everyday lives.

Point to the treasure map. **We need to remember that God is always with us—even when we're alone. By remembering that God never leaves us and is with us in our everyday lives, we can avoid the Great Lonely Desert. Which clue did we discover today?** Help children decide that today's lesson was, "We find God in our everyday lives" clue. Choose a child to take it off the *Use the Clues!* board and place it on the map.

Use the Clues!
(Bible Review)

Okay, let's see what you remember.

- **What places and situations do we find God in?** (children will have varied responses depending on the verses studied)
- **Why do we sometimes think God isn't with us?** (we don't look for Him in the place or situation, we forget about God)

- **How do we avoid the Great Lonely Desert?** (by remembering that God is with us in our everyday lives)
- **How can you encourage others who feel alone?** (by telling them God is with us in our everyday lives and sharing a verse from the Bible that reminds us of that)

At this point each week, go through *Use the Clues!* found in the *Resource* section to help children review the ways they can search for God. Go over all weeks up to this week.

BIBLE MEMORY WAYPOINT
(Scripture Memory)

Hebrews 13:5b

- *Objective: Children will hide God's Word in their hearts for guidance, protection, and encouragement.*

Read this week's memory verse from your Bible. Write it on the board and point to each word as you read it:

God has said, "Never will I leave you; never will I forsake you" (Hebrews 13:5b).

To help children memorize the Bible verse, enlist their help to make it a rebus. Ask children to come up one by one to erase words and replace them with pictures or symbols. For example, I could be an eye, leave could be a leaf, you could be U. After each replacement, read the verse together aloud.

PRAYER STATION

- **Objective:** *Children will explore and practice prayer for themselves in small groups.*
- **Materials:** *Copies of* StationMaster Card #4 *for each adult or teen helper*

Break into small groups of three to five children. Assign a teen or adult helper to each small group and give each helper a copy of *StationMaster Card #4* (see Resources, 95) with ideas for group discussion and prayer.

SNACK STOP: PRETZEL WORDS (Optional)

If you plan to provide a snack, this is an ideal time to serve it.

- **Materials:** *pretzel sticks, trail mix, small bowls*

Give each child a handful of pretzel sticks. Put trail mix in bowls within reach of children. Ask them to spell or make a picture with the pretzel sticks how they can see God in their life today. Helpers can assist younger children to spell as needed. Children can use the trail mix to add details to their words or pictures before consuming them.

Note: Always be aware of children with food allergies and have another option on hand if necessary.

APPLICATION

■ *Objective: Children will have opportunities to show how the lesson works in their own lives through activities and take-home papers.*

Some children's ministries may allow children to play outside at this point. If yours does not, choose one of the following activities.

Freeze Frames

This game lets children think about the ways God is with them in everyday situations and times. The children will cavort, dance, and hop around the play area until you call out a time of day or a place. Then they will freeze their bodies into a pose that shows something they might do at that time or place. Walk around and observe their frozen poses. Ask for explanations if you can't figure out what they're doing. To unfreeze, say, "Where is God?" They'll answer, "He's with us every day in every way," and then start moving around the room again.

Where Is God? Button

■ *Materials: Shrink plastic, baking trays, permanent markers, clear packing tape, scissors, safety pins*

Cut shrink plastic to size that will shrink to 3–4 inches. Write "Where is God?" on the board. Children will copy it onto their piece of shrink plastic and add designs. Follow directions on the package to shrink the plastic. After shrinking it, help them tape a safety pin to the back. Pin on their buttons and let them interact with each other and helpers to practice answering the question "Where is God?" Tell them by wearing the button this week, they can give others help in their search for God.

ON THE FAST TRACK! *(Take-Home Papers)*

(Optional) **Who would like to choose a prize from the treasure box?** Show the *On the Fast Track!* take-home papers. **In your *On the Fast Track!* paper, there are activities to do and a Bible verse to memorize. To earn a prize, complete all the activities at home and learn your verse. When you're finished, ask your parents or guardian to sign the ticket and bring it with you next week. If you do, you'll get to choose a prize from the treasure box!**

Distribute the take-home papers and notes about bringing clean trash next week just before children leave.

ALL ABOARD FOR BIBLE TRUTH STUDY VERSES
(Bible Discover and Learn Time)

1. Genesis 1:11–1

2. Genesis 1:24–25

3. Psalm 4:8

4. Psalm 23:1–4

5. Psalm 34:4

6. Psalm 40:1

7. Psalm 46:1

8. Psalm 84:11

9. Psalm 85:12

10. Psalm 147:8

11. 1 Timothy 4:4

12. 2 Timothy 3:16

Memory Verse:

Sing to the LORD, all the earth; proclaim his salvation day after day (1 Chronicles 16:23).

Note: Younger children may memorize the shorter version of this verse in bold print.

Bible Basis:

Genesis 1:11–14

Bible Truth:

We find God in His awesome creation.

You Will Need:

- ☐ treasure map mounted on a wall
- ☐ 1 poster board
- ☐ large quantity of clean "trash" such as cereal and juice boxes, paper, foil, paper towel rolls, milk jugs, etc.
- ☐ 7 rolls of masking or duct tape
- ☐ handfuls of fresh tree leaves and twigs
- ☐ *(Optional)* 1 potted tree
- ☐ treat jar
- ☐ *Use the Clues!* poster with map clues
- ☐ *On the Fast Track! #5* take-home paper
- ☐ *StationMaster Card #5*
- ☐ *(Optional)* treasure box
- ☐ *(Optional)* Snack: cut-up fruit such as apples, bananas or oranges
- ☐ *(Optional)* Activity #1: beanbag, small plush animal or block

When you see this icon, it means preparation will take more than five minutes.

🧳 GET SET!
(Lesson Preparation)

- ■ 🧭 Print today's Bible memory verse on a poster board: **Sing to the LORD, all the earth; proclaim his salvation day after day (1 Chronicles 16:23).** Hang the poster board on the wall.
- ■ Make a copy of *On the Fast Track #5* take-home paper for each child.
- ■ Make a copy of *StationMaster Card #5* for each helper.
- ■ Create seven piles of "clean trash" in an area of the room, along with one roll of tape per pile, one sheet of paper, and a marker.
- ■ Set out the treat jar and *(optional)* treasure box.
- ■ Set up snack or outside play activities if you include these items in your children's ministry.
- ■ If using optional Activity #2, print a copy of memory verses from past four lessons.

🎫 TICKETS PLEASE!
(Welcome and Bible Connection)

- ■ ***Objective:*** *To excite children's interest and connect their own life experiences with the Bible Truth, children will make trees to create a classroom forest.*

Welcome Time Activity: Forest Fabrication

■ *Materials: large sheets of paper, markers or crayons with many greens and browns, glue, handfuls of fresh leaves and twigs*

As children arrive, give each one a sheet of paper to draw a large tree of any sort. Encourage creativity. In addition to drawing, the children can glue on leaves and twigs to make their tree dimensional. Mount their creations on the wall to make a sort of forest.

When everyone has arrived, call children to the lesson area and welcome them. Offer them a treat from the treat jar. Say: **God likes it when children search Him out. Whenever they do, He rewards them by letting them find Him. The treats remind us of that reward.** Children may eat their treat or take it home.

(Optional) If children returned a signed Fast Track! ticket, they may choose a prize from the treasure box.

Sharing Time and Bible Connection

Introduce today's lesson by discussing these questions. As you talk, give every child an opportunity to say something. If you can go outside to see and touch trees near the church, do so as you introduce the lesson. Otherwise, have a sampling of different kinds of leaves or bark or pictures of trees the children would recognize.

■ **Who knows the names of the trees these leaves came from?**
■ **Why are trees important in our world?** (they provide habitat and food for animals, food for humans; we make things like wood, paper, crayons, medicine, and musical instruments from trees; provide jobs for people; make our world more beautiful)

What would we do without trees? There are thousands and thousands of kinds of trees in the world. Many kinds we don't even have in our city. Encourage children to touch the bark and leaves and notice the tiny details. Have them call out what they observe.

After this sharing time, help your students connect their discussion to the Bible story they are about to hear from Genesis 1:11–14:

No one has counted all the trees in the world, and I certainly don't know the names of them all. But I know one thing for sure: I couldn't make even one tree myself. Could you? Of course not. But I know who did! The trees and every other thing in nature are clues for us. We can use these clues in our search for God, because <u>we can find God in His awesome creation</u>.

ALL ABOARD FOR BIBLE TRUTH
(Bible Discover and Learn Time)

Genesis 1:11-14

- ◼ *Objective: Children will study Genesis 1:11–14 and recognize that God created nature and nature leads us to find God.*
- ◼ *Materials: Bible, seven piles of clean trash, seven rolls of tape, paper, markers, Use the Clues! poster with map clues.*

Everything you see—the ground you walk on and the air you breathe—was made by God. In the beginning of the world, God spoke and things happened. On the third day of the world, God said these words: Read them from Genesis 1:11 in your Bible. **"Let the land produce vegetation: seed-bearing plants and trees on the land that bear fruit." God made every kind of tree and plant in that moment, and then He decided something.** Read Genesis 1:12 from your Bible. **"God saw that it was good."**

Now this was just the third day of the whole week of creation. What other things did God make? Let children call out ideas. **In the first book of the Bible, Genesis, God tells us He made the light and the dark, water, sky and the ground, animals, birds, fish, and yes, people. Everything in nature was made by God Himself. And He told us He thought it was good.**

Today, we're going to design trees. Each group will have a pile of objects and a roll of tape they can use to make a tree. Divide the class into seven groups with a mix of older and younger children; assign each to a pile of "trash" with tape and a sheet of white paper.

After you create your tree, you will need to make up a name for it. Write the name on the paper and tape it to the tree. Allow 10 to 15 minutes for groups to design their trees. Have helpers assist where needed. Then ask each group to present their tree to the class.

Wow! The trees you made are amazing. You all did a great job. Give all the groups a hand for their work. **I love the details you put into your creation. It took us 15 minutes to make seven trees. How long did it take God to make every living tree?** (one day)

These trees are beautifully created. Now, if I want to praise the beauty and creativity of one of these trees (point to a tree) ***should I tell the tree, or should I tell the ones who made the tree?*** (let children respond) **I shouldn't talk to the tree, but to the group that made the tree.** Go to a group and say: **You guys did a great job. I like the way you wrapped the tape or glued the paper. What clever tree designers you are!**

The same is true with God. Should I go to one of God's beautiful trees (hold up a real leaf) **and say, "Wow! You are so unique. You are tall and strong and smell so good. You are amazing. I want to worship you"?** (no) **Of course not! Don't get confused! We don't worship trees, or any other thing God made. We worship God who made them.**

The world around us is like God's fingerprint. When you smell a

sweet fruit, or find a really cool snake, when you climb a rocky mountain or try to count the stars at night you experience more of who God is. All of creation gives us a pretty big clue in our search for God. Creation shows us God's glory. God's beautiful world shows us that He is creative and appreciates beauty. Nature shows us that He cares for us and provides us with food and shelter that we need. Our solar system with its asteroids, planets, and sun is pretty spectacular—and don't you think the one who made it is even more spectacular? <u>We find God as we see how awesome His creation is</u>.

Point to the treasure map. <u>God lets us find Him as we appreciate and enjoy nature</u>. On our search for God, we want to be protected from the Thunderstorm of Confusion. Which clue did we discover today? Help children decide that today's lesson was about the "We find God in His awesome creation" clue. Ask a volunteer to take it off the *Use the Clues!* board and place it on the map.

Use the Clues!
(Bible Review)

Use these questions to discuss today's lesson with your children.

- **What did God create?** (day, night, water, sky, ground, animals, people—everything there is!)
- **What did God say about what He made?** (it was good)
- **What does God's amazing creation tell us about Him?** (He is glorious, creative, loving. As we see how awesome each part of nature is, we realize that an even more awesome God created it all. Nature points us to Him.)
- **What is the best way to appreciate nature?** (worship God for making it, praise Him and thank Him, take care of what He's made)

At this point each week, follow the *Use the Clues!* found in the *Resource* section to help children review the Bible Truth and remember ways they can search for God. Review all weeks up to this week.

BIBLE MEMORY WAYPOINT   1 Chronicles 16:23
(Scripture Memory)

- **Objective:** *Children will hide God's Word in their hearts for guidance, protection, and encouragement.*

Read this week's memory verse from the poster. Point to each word as you read it:
Sing to the Lord, all the earth; proclaim his salvation day after day
(1 Chronicles 16:23).
Repeat each phrase several times until the verse is familiar to the children. Then, to

help them memorize the verse, play a pop-up game. Seat everyone in a circle. Choose a child to start by jumping up and saying the first word, then sitting down quickly. The next child should pop up, say the next word, then sit down. Continue in this way around the circle. You can vary this game by having each "popper" say two or three words at a time. Challenge kids to do it as quickly as possible with no mistakes

PRAYER STATION

■   *Objective: Children will explore and practice prayer for themselves in small groups.*
■ *Materials: Copies of* StationMaster Card #5 *for each adult or teen helper*

Break into small groups of three to five children. Assign a teen or adult helper to each group and give each helper a copy of *StationMaster Card #5* (see Resources, 95) with ideas for group discussion and prayer.

SNACK STOP: FRUIT OF THE LAND (Optional)

If you plan to provide a snack, this is an ideal time to serve it.

■ *Materials: cut up apples, bananas and/or oranges*

Set out plates of cut-up fruit and let children help themselves. Talk about their favorite foods that come from trees and other types of plants God created.
Note: Avoid strawberries and other foods typically associated with food allergies and have other options on hand.

APPLICATION

■ *Objective: Children will have opportunities to show how the lesson works in their own lives through activities and take-home papers.*

Some children's ministries may allow children to play outside at this point. If yours does not, choose one of the following activities.

Memory Verse Rehearse

■ *Materials: small plush toy, block or beanbag, printed copy of memory verses for weeks 1–4*

Help keep the memory verses fresh in children's hearts by reviewing this and the past four weeks of verses with this game. Divide into teams of 4 or 5. Have them stand side by side in their groups in a wide semi-circle. Put an object such as a beanbag, small plush toy, or block in the center of the semi-circle. Tell the children this is like a game show. You're the host and will ask questions about the verses they've learned these five weeks. If they think they know the answer they have to run to the object, pick it up, and run back to their team. The whole team can help the person correctly answer the question. Phrase the questions like this:

■ **What is the rest of this verse?** (read part of one verse)
■ **What verse goes with this reference?** (read only the reference)
■ **What verse tells us about friends?** (Proverbs 17:17)
■ **Which verse tells how we'll find God?** (Jeremiah 29:13)
■ **Fill in the missing words of this verse.** (read verse minus two key words)

Yea or Boo?

Review the Bible story and Bible Truth with this game. You'll make a statement. If it's true, children should jump up and down and yell, "Yea!" If it's not true, have them fall to their knees, slap the floor, and shout, "Boo!"

■ **God did an amazing job when He created all the trees.** *Yea!*
■ **God put lots of different details into each tree.** *Yea!*
■ **If you hurt a tree, Mother Nature will get mad.** *Boo! Ask why it's a boo.*
■ **God wants us to take care of His creations.** *Yea!*
■ **Trees are so amazing, they're like gods. O mighty tree! How majestic you are!** *Boo! Ask why it's a boo.*
■ **God came up with all the different types of trees all by himself.** *Yeah!*
■ **God lives inside trees. So to find God, you go hug a tree.** *Boo! Ask why not.*
■ **Anyone can make a tree or plant.** *Boo! Ask why it's a boo.*
■ **Only God can make trees, creatures and every other living thing.** *Yea!*

Add statements of your own if you choose, or have students suggest possible statements.

ON THE FAST TRACK! *(Take-Home Papers)*

(Optional) Produce the treasure box. **Are you going to get a chance at the treasure box next week? Okay! Take home this *On the Fast Track!* paper I'm going to hand out. When you've done the activities and memorized the Bible verse, ask your parents or guardian to sign the ticket. Bring it back next week and you'll get to choose a prize from the treasure box!**

Distribute the take-home papers just before children leave.

LESSON SIX: Seen Jesus?

Memory Verse:
God placed all things under [Jesus'] feet and **appointed [Jesus] to be the head over everything for the church** (Ephesians 1:22).
Note: Younger children may memorize the shorter version of this verse in bold print.

Bible Basis:
Psalm 51:15–17

Bible Truth:
We find God at church.

Geyser of Greatness

You Will Need:

- [ ] treasure map mounted on wall
- [ ] construction paper – white and assorted colors
- [ ] puppets
- [ ] Bible time dress-up box
- [ ] *(Optional)* instruments
- [ ] treat jar
- [ ] *Use the Clues!* poster with map clues
- [ ] *On the Fast Track! #6* take-home paper
- [ ] *StationMaster Card #6*
- [ ] *(Optional)* treasure box
- [ ] *(Optional)* Snack: dried fruit (golden and dark raisins, cranberries, apricots, or bag of mixed diced dried fruit), graham crackers or round snack crackers
- [ ] *(Optional)* Activity: several sheets of poster board

 When you see this icon, it means preparation will take more than five minutes.

GET SET!
(Lesson Preparation)

- ■ Print today's memory verse on a white board:
  God placed all things under [Jesus'] feet and appointed [Jesus] to be the head over everything for the church (Ephesians 1:22).
- ■ Make a copy of *On the Fast Track #6* take-home paper for each child.
- ■ Make a copy of *StationMaster Card #6* for each helper.
- ■ Set out the treat jar and *(optional)* treasure box.
- ■ Set up snack or outside play activities if you include these items in your children's ministry. Cut up dried fruit for snack if necessary.
- ■ Obtain any necessary permission if needed for optional Activity #2 ifyou are using it.

TICKETS PLEASE!
(Welcome and Bible Connection)

- ■ **Objective:** *To excite children's interest and connect their own life experiences with the Bible Truth, children will create a collage image of their church.*

Welcome Time Activity: Church Collage

■ *Materials:* white construction paper; construction paper in assorted colors, scissors, glue sticks

As children arrive, ask them to make a picture collage of your church. Have them cut squares, triangles, rectangles, or other shapes out of colored paper and glue these shapes onto the white construction paper background. They might make the church exterior, the sanctuary, your classroom, or any other part of the church.

When everyone has arrived, call children to the lesson area and welcome them. Offer them a treat from the treat jar. Say: **God likes it when children search for Him. When they do, He rewards them by letting you find Him. The treats remind us of that reward.** Children may eat their treat or take it home.

(Optional) If children returned a signed Fast Track! ticket, they may choose a prize from the treasure box.

Sharing Time and Bible Connection

Introduce today's lesson with this simple guessing game. As much as possible, give every child an opportunity to respond. After each clue, pause while kids guess. Congratulate the one who guesses you're talking about your church.

I'm going to describe a place. You can guess what it is when you think you know what I'm talking about.
This is a place in our town/city.
You'll find people here lots of days, but they don't stay overnight here.
People of all different ages come to this place.
There are many rooms, including a really big one.
People eat and play and learn in this place.
There are [number of pastors in your church] **leaders.**
People get married and baptized in this place.
Sometimes people sing here.

After this sharing time, help your students connect their discussion to the Bible story they are about to hear from Psalm 51:15-17:

Our church is someplace special. Lots of things happen here, like learning, worshiping, praying, enjoying other people's company, serving, giving, being forgiven, and healing. Another thing that happens at our church is that we can find God here. We won't see Him in a body, but <u>we still will find God at church</u>. Let's see how.

📖 ALL ABOARD FOR BIBLE TRUTH
(Bible Discover and Learn Time)

Psalm 51:15-17

- **Objective:** *Children will study Psalm 51:15–17 and understand what brings God to their church.*
- **Materials:** *pastor and worship dancer dress-up clothes, pretend microphones, instruments (optional) puppets, Bibles for the children, Use the Clues! poster with map clues.*

Note: This activity uses a somewhat traditional model of church. Feel free to adapt this activity to more closely reflect the model of your own church.

Choose one child to be the "pastor" and let him or her choose something from the dress-up box that resembles the pastor's garments. Pick several children to be the worship team or choir. Give them instruments (*optional*) and/or pretend microphones. Pick several other children to be worship dancers and let them choose outfits. Choose some children to be the puppet team, and give them puppets. Remaining children should sit in chairs as the congregation. Give the groups 5 minutes and instruct them to decide how to act out two kinds of church services: One where they glorify God in their roles, and the other where they glorify themselves. For example:

Pastor:
Not Glorifying: Pastor can tell the congregation what a good person he is.
Glorifying: "What an incredible God we have! Let's read what the Bible says about Him."

Worship Team:
Not Glorifying: Push to be the front person while singing or playing an instrument.
Glorifying: Everybody sings a praise song together and works together.

Dance Ministry:
Not Glorifying: Each tries to outdo the others, hogs the stage.
Glorifying: Do a simple dance together to "Jesus Loves Me."

Puppet Team:
Not Glorifying: Fight over the puppets and who gets to be the star.
Glorifying: Puppets present a Bible story.

Congregation:
Not Glorifying: Play, talk during the service, or not pay attention.
Glorifying: Have the group listen, take notes, look at their Bibles or pastor.

Okay, let's start with the wrong kind of church service that does not glorify God. Cue the various actors to play out their roles. **Do you think that God was in that service?** (no)

Let's see a church service where the people want to glorify God. Let the worship team/choir, dancers, puppet team, pastor, and congregation repeat their performance, but as people glorifying God. **Why do you think that God was in that service?** Have children put down their props and sit down.

Ask children with Bibles to open them to Psalm 51. They can share with others as appropriate. **David, who was a shepherd and then a king, wrote Psalm 51. He made a very bad choice and realized he had messed up. So David talked to God about it. He asked God to open his lips so that he could praise God. He said, "God, you don't rejoice when we sacrifice or bring you offerings or I would do that. What you want is a broken and contrite heart. You want me to show I'm sorry for my wrong doing."**

You see, God doesn't want people to come to church to make themselves look good. God wants our hearts to be quiet and listening to Him while we're in church. When we sing or pray or serve in church to please Him, we can be sure He is in our church with us. He has a special way of talking to us through the Bible and other people when our minds are thinking about Him. When our thoughts remain on Him and our actions are pleasing to Him, then <u>we find that God is present at our church</u>.

Point to the treasure map. **If we're humble and listen and choose to honor Him with the way we worship, <u>we'll find God at church</u> with us. When we love God and love others He will be there with us and we can duck out of the way of the Geyser of Greatness. Which clue did we discover today?** Help children decide that today's lesson was about the "God is present at our church" clue. Choose a child to take it off the *Use the Clues!* board and place it on the map.

Use the Clues!
(Bible Review)

Okay, let's see what you remember.

- **How do we find God at church?** (by being a ready listener, doing our worship to please Him and not to make ourselves look good or impress people)
- **Why do we want to duck out of the way of the Geyser of Greatness?** (because being in church is a time to be humble and

let God shine, not ourselves, it's about Him, not us)

- **When you're sitting in church next time, how can you find God there?** (listen to what's happening in the service, tell God in your heart that you want to hear and find Him, pay attention to the music and sermon instead of the people around yo)

At this point, follow the *Use the Clues!* found in the *Resource* section. Use the treasure map and clues to help children review the Bible Truth and remember ways they can search for God. Review all weeks up to this week.

BIBLE MEMORY WAYPOINT   EPHESIANS 1:22
(Scripture Memory)

■ **Objective:** *Children will hide God's Word in their hearts for guidance, protection, and encouragement.*

Read this week's memory verse from your Bible. Write it on the white board and read it with the children:

> **God placed all things under [Jesus'] feet and appointed [Jesus] to be head over everything for the church (Ephesians 1:22).**

To help children memorize the Bible verse, erase two key words and have the class read it. Let a volunteer erase another word or two, then ask everyone to recite it again. Continue having different children erase words, followed by another recitation, until most or all of the words are gone.

PRAYER STATION

■ **Objective:** *Children will explore and practice prayer for themselves in small groups.*
■ **Materials:** *Copies of* StationMaster Card #6 *for each adult or teen helper*

Break into small groups of three to five children. Assign a teen or adult helper to each small group and give each helper a copy of *StationMaster Card #6* (see Resources, 96) with ideas for group discussion and prayer.

SNACK STOP: STAINED GLASS CRACKERS (Optional)

If you plan to provide a snack, this is an ideal time to serve it.

■ **Materials:** *dried fruit (golden and dark raisins, cranberries, apricots, or bag of mixed diced dried fruit), graham crackers or round snack crackers*

Cut large pieces of dried fruit into smaller pieces. Using a cracker as the base, have children design a stained glass window with the different colored fruits. If your class doesn't know what a stained glass window is, show a picture and tell how these windows decorate many churches.

Note: Always be aware of children with food allergies and have another option on hand if necessary.

APPLICATION

■ **Objective:** *Children will have opportunities to show how the lesson works in their own lives through activities and take-home papers.*

Some children's ministries may allow children to play outside at this point. If yours does not, choose one of the following activities.

 Seen Jesus? Posters

Divide children into small groups. Give each group a large poster board. Challenge them to create a "Seen Jesus?" poster that they'll hang in the church. The poster should spark people to think toward noticing the presence of Christ among them wherever they are in the church. After writing "Seen Jesus?" prominently on the posters, they can use their creativity to decorate them. Gain permission ahead of time for children to put up their posters in various areas of the facility.

 Church Prayer Walk

Divide the class into a couple of groups if the class is large, otherwise you can travel as one group. Explain that you are going to walk around the church and pray for people to be aware that God is present in every aspect of the church's activities and life. To make this more child-friendly, you can assign pairs of children to be leaders for different segments of the prayer walk, leading the group of walking and then praying in one place. Try to prayer walk throughout as many sections of the church as you can: sanctuary, nursery, kitchen, fellowship areas, classrooms, offices, etc.

 ON THE FAST TRACK! *(Take-Home Papers)*

(Optional) **Who can explain how to get a prize from the treasure box?** Let a volunteer explain how it works. Show the *On the Fast Track!* take-home papers. **That's right. When you do the activities and learn the verse in your *On the Fast Track!* paper this week, all you need to do is ask your parents or guardian to sign the ticket. When you bring it next week, you'll get to choose a prize from the treasure box!**

Distribute the take-home papers just before children leave.

LESSON SEVEN: Look All Around You

Trash Heap of Heartlessness

Memory Verse:
The King will reply, "I tell you the truth, **whatever you did for one of the least of these brothers of mine, you did for me**" (Matthew 25:40).
Note: Younger children may memorize the shorter version of this verse in bold print.

Bible Basis:
Luke 10:30–37

Bible Truth:
We can find God anywhere and everywhere.

You Will Need:

- ☐ treasure map mounted on a wall
- ☐ large map of the world, country, or state
- ☐ soft objects to throw such as craft pom-poms
- ☐ poster board
- ☐ Bible time dress-up box
- ☐ (Optional) stick horse
- ☐ treat jar
- ☐ *Use the Clues!* poster with map clues
- ☐ *On the Fast Track! #7* paper
- ☐ *StationMaster Card #7*
- ☐ (Optional) treasure box
- ☐ (Optional) Snack: pretzel sticks, raisins or chocolate chips/candy-coated chocolates
- ☐ (Optional) Activity #1: sticks (such as brooms or yard sticks)
- ☐ (Optional) Activity #2: newspapers and/or magazines with stories of people helping others, puppets

 When you see this icon, it means preparation will take more than five minutes.

 GET SET!
(Lesson Preparation)

- ■ Print today's memory verse on a poster board: **The King will reply, "I tell you the truth, whatever you did for one of the least of these brothers of mine, you did for me" (Matthew 25:40)**
- ■ Make a copy of *On the Fast Track #7* take-home paper for each child.
- ■ Make a copy of *StationMaster Card #7* for each helper.
- ■ Set out the treat jar and *(optional)* treasure box.
- ■ Set up snack or outside play activities if you include these items in your children's ministry.
- ■ Mount the map for the welcome activity if you're using it.

 TICKETS PLEASE!
(Welcome and Bible Connection)

- ■ **Objective:** *To excite children's interest and connect their own life experiences with the Bible Truth, children will play a game and consider how many places there are in the world.*

Welcome Time Activity: Geo Darts

■ *Materials: large map of the world, country, or state, soft objects such as craft pom-poms*

Hang the map on the wall. Have it as close to eye level for the children as possible. On the white board, print the capital letters of the alphabet. Children will take turns tossing a pom-pom at the map. A helper should stand at the map and note where it hits, then state the place name at that spot. Cross off or erase the first letter of that name from your alphabet list. Challenge the children to erase as many letters as possible. Chat about how many places there are that they haven't visited or even heard of.

When everyone has arrived, call children to the lesson area and welcome them. Offer them a treat from the *treat jar*. Say: **Why do you think I want to give you a treat today? It's because you being here today is sweet to God. He's pleased when children want to find Him. He rewards their search for Him with His presence.** Children may eat their treat or take it home.

(Optional) If children returned a signed Fast Track! ticket, they may choose a prize from the treasure box.

Sharing Time and Bible Connection

Introduce today's lesson by discussing these questions.

We know we can see God in our family and friends. We can also see His love and creativity in the world around us and in nature. Last week, we found out that God is here right now, today, in our church.

Let's pretend you got on a plane and flew to the other side of the world. What place would you want to visit?

■ **Would God be on the other side of the world, too?** (yes)

■ **Where do you think you could travel in the world and not find God?**

■ **How do you know God would be everywhere else in the world?** (the Bible says so)

After this sharing time, help your students connect their discussion to the Bible story they are about to hear from Luke 10.

Let's find out just what the Bible says and see if you are right!

ALL ABOARD FOR BIBLE TRUTH   Luke 10:30-37
(Bible Discover and Learn Time)

■ *Objective:* Children will study Luke 10:30–37 and hear how a man cared for a stranger in a faraway land, an example of how God is found in all places near and far.

■ *Materials:* Bible time dress-up box, stick horse (optional), Use the Clues! poster with map clues.

Bring out the dress up box. **Who would like to help act out the Bible story today? I'll read it from the Bible while some of you act as the people in the story.** Select volunteers to play a hurt man, priest, Levite, Samaritan, innkeeper, and three robbers. After putting on their costumes, put the Samaritan, priest, Levite, and hurt man on the right side of the classroom, the robbers in the center, and the innkeeper on the left.

After familiarizing yourself with the text here, read the pertinent facts from your Bible for the class. The actors will silently dramatize what you read.

A man was going down from Jerusalem to Jericho, (the soon-to-be hurt man rides across the front of the room as if on a horse) **when he fell into the hands of robbers.** (The robbers jump out at the Samaritan and gently pretend to knock him to the ground.) **They stripped him of his clothes, beat him, and went away.** (Robbers act this out.) **They left the beat-up man lying at the side of the road.**

A priest was traveling down the same road a little later. (Priest walks across the front of the room.) **He saw the wounded man. But he just went to the other side of the road and kept going.** (Priest moves away from the man and hurry away.) **Next a Levite, who was a Jewish worker in the synagogue, came along. He saw the hurt man too.** (The Levite walks across the front of the room). **But he just walked around him.** (Levite does this.)

The hurt man just lay there. He couldn't get up, couldn't get help. Later in the day, a Samaritan man came traveling down the road. (Samaritan rides the stick horse across the front of the room.) **When he saw the hurt man, he felt bad for him. He went over to him and bandaged his wounds, pouring on oil and wine.** (The Samaritans acts this out.) **Then he put the man on his own animal.** (Samaritan puts the man on his stick horse.) **But he didn't stop there. He took him to an inn, and asked the innkeeper to take care of him.** (They go to the innkeeper.) **The next day the Samaritan gave the innkeeper two silver coins to pay for the man's care.** (Samaritan gives coins to the innkeeper.) **"Look after him,"** he said, **"and when I return, I'll pay you for any extra expense you may have."**

Let's give our actors and actresses a great big hand. Volunteers can take off their costumes and sit down. **Isn't it amazing that this Samaritan not only helped a stranger, but also took care of him for days? You might have heard that story before. God put that story in the Bible because it shows us how He wants us to treat others. When God lives in us and others who follow Jesus as their Lord, we will care for**

others the way God does. That's how <u>we can find God any place in the world</u>.

Point to the treasure map. **When people in any part of the world help live the way God wants, they care for others. God is found there. Living that way keeps us away from the stink of the Trash Heap of Heartlessness. That's where the priest and Levite were. But we can avoid it. Which clue did we discover today?** Help children decide that today's lesson was about the "God is everywhere" clue. Choose a child to take it off the *Use the Clues!* board and place it on the map.

Use the Clues!
(Bible Review)

Okay, let's see what you remember.

- **How did the Samaritan man show that God was on that lonely road with the wounded man?** (he showed kindness and cared for the man the way God would have)
- **Could this kind of story happen in other places in the world?** (yes) **How?** (anyone who knows Jesus as their Lord can act in godly caring toward others, and in that care people find God)

- **Name some ways you can care for people who need help?** (be kind, share what you have with others who need it, speak up for what is right)
- **Name some places outside of our town where you could find God this week?** (Answers will vary: anywhere and everywhere, when we live the way God wants and when other believers do the same)

At this point, follow the *Use the Clues!* found in the *Resource* section. Use the treasure map and clues to help children review the Bible Truth and remember ways they can search for God. Review all weeks up to this week.

BIBLE MEMORY WAYPOINT   Matthew 25:40
(Scripture Memory)

- *Objective: Children will hide God's Word in their hearts for guidance, protection, and encouragement.*

Read this week's memory verse from the poster board:

The King will reply, "I tell you the truth, whatever you did for one of the least of these brothers of mine, you did for me" (Matthew 25:40).

To help children memorize the Bible verse, say it phrase by phrase. Say the first segment with the children repeating it. Add the second segment, so children repeat both. Add a third segment, so children say all three. Continue to the end. Then rehearse it in groups. Call out a category, such as girls, boys, kids wearing blue, blond haired people, eight year olds, etc. Children falling in the category stand where they are and say the verse together, then sit down. Repeat with a new category. Make some silly too.

PRAYER STATION

- **Objective:** *Children will explore and practice prayer for themselves in small groups.*
- **Materials:** *Copies of* StationMaster Card #7 *for each adult or teen helper*

Break into groups of three to five children. Assign a teen or adult helper to each small group and give each helper a copy of *StationMaster Card #7* (see Resources, 96) with ideas for group discussion and prayer.

SNACK STOP: COMPASS POINTS (Optional)

If you plan to provide a snack, this is an ideal time to serve it.

- **Materials:** *pretzel sticks, raisins or chocolate chips*

Point out the compass rose on the map from today's Welcome Time Activity and tell children they are going to make a compass to eat for a snack. Show children how to make a compass with pretzel sticks by making a plus sign using two or three sticks laid end to end up and down, and then perpendicular across. Give each child a small handful of raisins or chocolate chips. Tell them to show a direction (such as north, south, east, west) on their compass by laying a raisin at the point. Have older children help younger ones. After the four compass points have been found, let them start eating their snack while you all talk about places north, east, south, and west that children have visited or heard about.

Note: Always be aware of children with food allergies and have another option on hand if necessary.

APPLICATION

■ **Objective:** *Children will have opportunities to show how the lesson works in their own lives through activities and take-home papers.*

Some children's ministries may allow children to play outside at this point. If yours does not, choose one of the following activities.

 ## Samaritan Relay

■ **Materials:** *sticks (such as brooms or yard sticks)*

Divide into two or more teams. You'll need at least four people per team (more is better). Have half of each team go to the opposite side of the play area. These are the wounded people. Those on the other end are the Samaritans. Give the first Samaritan on each team a stick. He "rides" it like a stick horse to the wounded player end, where a waiting teammate gets on the "horse" and rides back with him. They both hop off and the next Samaritan rides away to pick up a wounded man teammate.

 ## What If? Puppet Skits

■ **Materials:** *current newspaper and/or magazines with stories of people helping others, puppets*

Break into small groups. Give each group a current newspaper or magazine with a story of people helping others, such as after a natural disaster. Also give each group two or more puppets. Ask a good reader to read the article (or a portion you've highlighted) aloud. The group will decide how followers of Jesus would show care to those in need and create a short puppet skit. After 10 minutes of reading and preparation, groups can present their puppet plays to the class.

 ### ON THE FAST TRACK! *(Take-Home Papers)*

(Optional) **Who wants to choose a prize from the treasure box?** Show the *On the Fast Track!* take-home papers. **In your *On the Fast Track!* paper, you'll see activities to do and a Bible verse to memorize. To earn a prize, do the activities at home this week and learn your verse. Ask your parents or guardian to sign the ticket and bring it next week. That's how you can choose a prize from the treasure box!**

Distribute the take-home papers just before children leave.

Reminder: Before you distribute today's take-home papers, take a moment to write the date of your last class for this program on the space provided!

LESSON EIGHT: Afraid? Who, Me?

Bog of Fear

Memory Verse:
I will trust and not be afraid. The LORD, the LORD is my strength and my song (Isaiah 12:2).

Bible Basis:
1 Kings 19:1–18

Bible Truth:
We find God in times when we're afraid.

You Will Need:

- [ ] treasure map mounted on a wall
- [ ] play dough
- [ ] poster board
- [ ] sound-making props such as crackly paper or brittle cellophane, wooden blocks, aluminum foil pans
- [ ] treat jar
- [ ] *Use the Clues!* poster with map clues
- [ ] *On the Fast Track! #8* take-home paper
- [ ] *StationMaster Card #8*
- [ ] *(Optional)* treasure box
- [ ] *(Optional)* Snack: pita bread or flour tortillas, jam or butter (optional), water
- [ ] *(Optional)* Activity #1: pictures of trees
- [ ] *(Optional)* Activity #2: 8" x 11" stiff acrylic transparency sheets cut in half, string, hole punch

 When you see this icon, it means preparation will take more than five minutes.

 ## GET SET!
(Lesson Preparation)

- ■ Print today's memory verse on a poster board:
  I will trust and not be afraid. The LORD, the LORD is my strength and my song (Isaiah 12:2).
- ■ Make a copy of *On the Fast Track #8* take-home paper for each child.
- ■ Make a copy of *StationMaster Card #8* for each helper.
- ■ Set out the treat jar and *(optional)* treasure box.
- ■ Set up snack or outside play activities if you include these items in your children's ministry.
- ■ Draw or cut out pictures of two or more trees and mount on paper for optional Activity #1 if using.

TICKETS PLEASE!
(Welcome and Bible Connection)

■ ***Objective:*** *To excite children's interest and connect their own life experiences with the Bible Truth, children create play dough scenes that remind them of times they've been afraid.*

Welcome Time Activity: Play Dough Scenes

■ *Materials: play dough*

Set out play dough and let children create scenes of times when they've been afraid. Ask helpers to chat with children about what they've created.

When everyone has arrived, gather children into the lesson area. Welcome them and offer a treat from the *treat jar*. Say: **God likes it when children search for Him. Whenever they do, He rewards them with His presence. The treats remind us of that reward.** Children may eat their treat now or take it home.

(*Optional*) If children returned a signed Fast Track! ticket, they may choose a prize from the treasure box.

Sharing Time and Bible Connection

Introduce today's lesson by discussing these questions. As you talk, give every child an opportunity to say something.

- **What kinds of things are you afraid of?** (If children are reluctant to share, start them off by telling a couple of things you yourself fear.)
- **Can you tell about a time you were afraid?**
- **What do you do when you feel afraid?** (look for Mom or Dad, pray)

Everyone, even adults, have times when they're afraid. Do you think Bible time people had moments of fear? They sure did! Today we're going to explore a time one of God's prophets was afraid. I wonder if <u>God was there during that time of fear</u>**. What do you think?** (Let children respond.) **Let's listen to our Bible story and find out!**

 # ALL ABOARD FOR BIBLE TRUTH   1 Kings 19:1–18
(Bible Discover and Learn Time)

- **Objective:** *Children will study 1 Kings 19:1–18 and discover that Elijah experienced God during a time when he was afraid.*
- **Materials:** *sound-making props such as crackly paper or brittle cellophane, wooden blocks, aluminum foil pans, Use the Clues! poster with map clues.*

Today we'll need everyone to help make the sound effects for our Bible story. Divide the class into three groups, and ask an older child to be the leader of each group. Assign several sounds to each group. Provide an assortment of objects to help them create sound effects. Sounds: angry queen, whiny Elijah, gulping and chewing sounds, snoring, footsteps, wind, earthquake, fire. Give groups a few minutes to decide how to make their sound effects. Tell them when you motion to a group at the appropriate moment, they should make the sound that matches what you're saying. You might want to give the group leaders a sign naming that group's sound effects to identify them for you.

Even famous people in the Bible had their times of fear. Elijah was the prophet who had faced 450 prophets of the false god Baal. And because he served the one true God, he won and they all died. But right after that, Elijah found himself alone. Then he got a frightening message. Queen Jezebel, was really mad because her

false prophets had lost to God and Elijah (angry queen sound effect).

She promised Elijah she was going to do the same thing to him as he had done to her prophets—kill him! Now Elijah was afraid. He forgot God was on his side and he ran for his life. He ran out into the desert, hoping he could escape the **angry queen** (running footsteps).

After a long hot run through the wilderness, Elijah was tired. He was discouraged. He felt really afraid. So he plopped down under a broom tree and prayed. This was not the prayer you might think. Elijah told God, "I've had enough, God. Just let me die." Then, feeling so tired from running for his life, he fell asleep (snoring sounds).

But suddenly, something woke Elijah up! Was it the queen's soldiers? No, it was an angel, who touched him and said, "Get up and eat." Elijah looked around. There by his head was a cake of bread baked on hot stones, and a jar of water. He ate and drank (gulping and chewing sounds). **Then he fell asleep again.** Once again, an angel came and touched him and told him to eat some more. There was more bread and water, so once again Elijah got up and ate and drank. Those two meals gave Elijah enough energy to start walking again (walking footstep sounds). **For 40 days and nights Elijah traveled through the wilderness to the mountain of God.** When he found a cave, he decided to stay there for the night.

The next day, God asked, "What are you doing here, Elijah?" Elijah whined (whining sound). **"Lord God, I've had it. Your people have turned away from you. I'm the only prophet left they haven't killed. Now they're trying to kill me too."**

"Go outside and stand before me," God commanded. Elijah felt afraid again, but he obeyed.

Suddenly a great and powerful wind whipped by (wind sound). **Elijah had to grab onto the rocks of the mountain to keep from being blown away!** Then a huge **earthquake shook the whole mountain** (earthquake sound). **Finally, a bright fire lit up the sky** (fire sound) **and then there was silence** (pause for a moment). **Then he heard a gentle whisper. Which do you think was God's voice?** Let children respond. **All of them were! God was in the wind and the earthquake and the fire to show Elijah that He was right there, even though Elijah was so afraid.**

"You are not the only one left who's serving me," God said. "There are 7,000 others who haven't bowed down to the false god Baal." Then God gave Elijah a new job. He sent him to choose two new kings and find a new prophet who would carry on Elijah's work.

Point to the treasure map. **Like Elijah, you and I have times when we're afraid. Does God go away in the scary times? No way! Elijah found out that God was there even when he was afraid. God is with us in our scary times too, even if we forget Him. When you and I are scared, we can call out for God. He'll be there. Calling out for God instead of staying afraid is how we leap over the Bog of Fear. Which clue did we discover today?**

Help children decide that today's lesson was about the "We find God in times when we're afraid" clue. Choose a child to take it off the *Use the Clues!* board and place it on the map.

Use the Clues!
(Bible Review)

Use these questions to discuss today's lesson with your class.

■ **Why was Elijah afraid?** (Queen Jezebel was angry and said she would kill him)

■ **What did Elijah do when he became afraid?** (he ran away, whined to God, gave up)

■ **How did God show Elijah He was right there with him in his scary time?** (first God sent an angel with food and water, then He talked to Elijah through wind, an earthquake, fire, and a whisper, He gave Elijah a new job)

■ **How can you find God the next time something scary happens to you?** (Children will have various responses, such as look for ways God shows He's there, pray, listen for God's voice, wait.)

Take some time, now, to follow the *Use the Clues!* found in the *Resource* section. Use the treasure map and clues to help children review the Bible Truths so far and remember ways they can search for God.

BIBLE MEMORY WAYPOINT   Isaiah 12:2
(Scripture Memory)

■ *Objective: Children will hide God's Word in their hearts for guidance, protection, and encouragement.*

Read this week's memory verse from the poster board. Point to each word as you read it:

I will trust and not be afraid. The LORD, the LORD is my strength and my song (Isaiah 12:2).

To help the children memorize the verse, divide the class in half and have the two groups face each other. One group will say a portion of the verse and the other group will echo it. Continue in this way through the whole verse, then reverse roles. Let them repeat the verse using high and low voices, singsong voices, etc.

PRAYER STATION

- **Objective:** *Children will explore and practice prayer for themselves in small groups.*
- **Materials:** *Copies of* StationMaster Card #8 *for each adult or teen helper*

Break into small groups of three to five children. Assign a teen or adult helper to each small group and give each helper a copy of *StationMaster Card #8* (see Resources, 97) with ideas for group discussion and prayer.

SNACK STOP: ELIJAH'S MEAL (Optional)

If you plan to provide a snack, this is an ideal time to serve it.

- **Materials:** *pita bread or flour tortillas, jam or butter (optional), water*

Ask the children to retell the part of the story where Elijah falls asleep under the tree. Then serve them the pita bread or tortillas as Elijah's bread, and cups of water.

Note: Always be aware of children with food allergies and have another option on hand if necessary.

APPLICATION

- **Objective:** *Children will have opportunities to show how the lesson works in their own lives through activities and take-home papers.*

Some children's ministries may allow children to play outside at this point. If yours does not, choose one of the following activities.

Elijah's Relay

■ *Materials: tree pictures (one per team)*

Divide into two or more teams. Set up the relay by mounting the tree pictures on the opposite side of the play area. Have teams line up behind a starting line. At your signal, the first player on each team races to the picture and tags it, then races back and tags the next player in their team who then races to the tree. The team whose players all tag the tree and return first wins.

 Disappear Fear! Sun Catcher

■ *Materials: 8" x 11" stiff acrylic transparency sheets cut in half, string, markers, hole punch*

The children will make sun catchers to remind them God is present with them when they're afraid. Have them write the first portion of the memory verse on the transparency: "I will trust and not be afraid." Then, add border designs with markers. They (or helpers) can punch two holes along the top and tie on a string hanger.

 ON THE FAST TRACK! *(Take-Home Papers)*

(Optional) **Who wants to choose a prize from the treasure box?** Show the *On the Fast Track!* take-home papers. **In your *On the Fast Track!* paper there are activities to do and a Bible verse to memorize. To earn a prize, complete all the activities at home and learn your verse. Ask your parents or guardian to sign the ticket on the front and bring it next week. If you do, you'll get to choose a prize from the treasure box!**

Distribute the take-home papers just before children leave.

Memory Verse:

The LORD lives! Praise be to my Rock! Exalted be God, the Rock, my Savior! (2 Samuel 22:47). *Note: Younger children may memorize the shorter version of this verse in bold print.*

Bible Basis:

2 Samuel 22;
Psalm 150

Bible Truth:

We find God in the middle of our excitement.

Footholds of Remembrance

You Will Need:

- ☐ treasure map mounted on a wall
- ☐ balloons
- ☐ 1 large poster board (28" x 22")
- ☐ 1 small, colored poster board (22" x 14")
- ☐ treat jar
- ☐ *Use the Clues!* poster with map clues
- ☐ *On the Fast Track! #9* take-home paper
- ☐ *StationMaster Card #9*
- ☐ (Optional) treasure box
- ☐ (Optional) Snack: ice cream cones, pudding, plastic spoons
- ☐ (Optional) Activity #2: card stock or poster board, glitter glue, markers or crayons, crepe paper, scissors, thin dowels, wide, strong tape

 When you see this icon, it means preparation will take more than five minutes.

 ## GET SET!

(Lesson Preparation)

- ■ ⏱ Print 2 Samuel 22:47 on the small colored poster board so the words use the entire board. **The LORD lives! Praise be to my Rock! Exalted be God, the Rock, my Savior! (2 Samuel 22:47).** Make a frame from the larger poster board by centering the small board on it and tracing the outer edge. Cut the colored board into 12 jigsaw puzzle pieces. Assemble the jigsaw pieces within the frame and trace each puzzle piece. Hang the framed puzzle poster in the classroom.
- ■ ⏱ Blow up and tie enough balloons for one for each child.
- ■ Make a copy of *On the Fast Track #9* take-home paper for each child.
- ■ Make a copy of *StationMaster Card #9* for each helper.
- ■ Set out the treat jar and *(optional)* treasure box.
- ■ Set up snack or outside play activities if you include these items in your children's ministry.
- ■ ⏱ Cut cardstock or poster board into elongated triangles for praise banners, if using optional Activity #2.

 ## TICKETS PLEASE!

(Welcome and Bible Connection)

- ■ *Objective: To excite children's interest and connect their own life experiences with the Bible Truth, children will create balloon faces and talk about what is exciting to them.*

Welcome Time Activity: Funny Face Balloons

■ *Materials: balloons, markers*

Have students draw a funny face on a balloon (or two different faces on two sides). Encourage them to add details to their faces. Helpers can work with younger children and get the children talking about the excitement that often comes when balloons are used, such as at parties and celebrations.

When everyone has arrived, welcome the children and offer them a treat from the treat jar. Say: **God is excited that you are here and so am I. Let's celebrate with a treat from our treat jar.** Children may eat their treat now or take it home.

(Optional) If children returned a signed Fast Track! ticket, they may choose a prize from the treasure box.

Sharing Time and Bible Connection

Introduce today's lesson with a mini-drama. Delegate this to a helper or perform it yourself. Build excitement by sounding thrilled and full of anticipation.

I won. I won! They had a contest at work/school, and they drew my name. Now I get to go to my favorite amusement park and stay in their hotel for five days. I get to go to the beach, the stores, and get all my meals free. I am so excited! What do I need to do? Let's see. I need to pack my clothes, and ask my neighbor to watch my dog, and pack my favorite shoes, and, um, what else? Look to kids and ask if they can think of anything you forgot. Hold up your Bible. **Should I take my Bible. Hmm, I don't think I have room. I'll read it when I get home . . . I can't believe I get to go!** Run out of the classroom as you wave goodbye.

After the mini-drama, help your students connect it to the Bible story from Psalm 150 and 2 Samuel 22:

What just happened? (Name of helper) **had such a wild and exciting thing happen, didn't he/she? What exciting thing has happened to you?** Let several children share briefly. **Have you ever noticed that when something really exciting happens, we can forget some things . . . and even Someone? David from the Old Testament had some really exciting times. He fought a lion and a bear, he fought a giant, he was chased by a king, and he won battles. Let's take a look at what King David did when he was excited.**

📖 ALL ABOARD FOR BIBLE TRUTH   2 Samuel 22; Psalm 150
(Bible Discover and Learn Time)

- ◾ **Objective:** *Children will study 2 Samuel 22 and Psalm 150 to learn that David saw God even in his most exciting times.*
- ◾ **Materials:** *six Bibles, Use the Clues! poster with map clues*

What do you know about David? (he fought a bear and a lion and won, he fought a giant and won, he was pursued by Saul, he was chosen to be king)

David was a smart, strong, and mighty warrior. He was good at lots of things. As a warrior, he fought many battles. Let children briefly pretend to sword fight. **Imagine how exciting it would be to fight and win so many battles.**

After one battle, David was so excited that he and his men had won. He could have told everyone how great he was or how amazing his soldiers were. He could have bragged about his strength and how well he commanded others. But he did something else.

David knew that he and his men didn't win the battle because they were stronger, or smarter. He remembered that they won because God gave them the ability to win. Even in all his excitement, David could see that God was a big part of what was happening.

David was a musician and a songwriter. So he made up a song about how God was with him in the fight. We can read that song in 2 Samuel 22. Open your Bible and read from verse 2: **"Lord, you are my deliverer."** Direct the children to stand and shout back those words to you like a cheer. **David said, "Death was all around me, but God caused our arrows to defeat the enemy."** Have the class shout, **"God, you saved my life." David exclaimed, "God is strong, and righteous, and perfect."** Have the class shout those words.

He ended his victory song by saying that in his excitement he would praise God, because God had given him victory. David also wrote another song that praised <u>God for being with him when he was excited</u>. We're going to read that one together.

Divide the children into six groups, making sure there is a Bible and a confident reader and writer in each group. Assign each group a verse from Psalm 150. Group members will work together to dramatically interpret the verse while one person (or the whole group) narrates, sings, or raps, the words. Allow 5–10 minutes for groups to decide how to demonstrate their verse, then let groups present their verses in the order of the psalm.

Everyone did a great job of praising God. If we do that when we're excited, we too will find <u>God in the middle of our excited times</u> in life.

Point to the treasure map. **God gives us the good things in our lives. When we enjoy these things, we want to remember who gave them to us. If we praise God for exciting times, we're stepping into the Footholds of Remembrance. If you try to climb up a steep rock, you need to find places for your feet. Those are called footholds. Remembering that God is right there in the excitement is like finding** the right places to put our feet as we travel toward the treasure.

Which clue did we discover today? Help children decide that today's lesson was about the "God is with us when we are excited" clue. Choose a child to take it off the *Use the Clues!* board and place it on the map.

Use the Clues!
(Bible Review)

Okay, let's see what you remember.

■ **What kind of person was David?** (strong, courageous, a songwriter and musician, a king)

■ **What kind of excitement did David have in 2 Samuel?** (God helped him win a battle over his enemies)

■ **Where was God in David's exciting time?** (He was right there with him, God made the exciting time happen)

■ **How did David honor God who gave him the ability to win the battle?** (he wrote a song of celebration that talked about how God had helped him)

■ **How do you think you might see God when you're in the middle of an exciting situation?** Children will have various responses.

David didn't forget about God when he was so excited. He saw God as a part of the excitement, and he praised God. You and I probably won't be in a battle like David, but we have our own exciting times. And we can remember that <u>God is right there in the middle of it with us</u>.

Take some time now to use the treasure map and clues to review the Bible Truths children have learned thus far. Talk about ways kids can search for God.

BIBLE MEMORY WAYPOINT   2 Samuel 22:47
(Scripture Memory)

■ **Objective:** *Children will hide God's Word in their hearts for guidance, protection, and encouragement.*

Read this week's memory verse from the framed puzzle poster. Use voice inflections to make the statements emphatic.

The LORD lives! Praise be to my Rock! Exalted be God, the Rock, my Savior! (2 Samuel 22:47).

Have the children divide into three groups. Each group will say one phrase when you point to it. Move from group to group to have them state the verse in correct order. Then have half the children go outside or hide their eyes while the other half hides the twelve pieces. Those outside will search for the pieces and put them in the puzzle frame. Lead everyone to recite the verse together, then let the groups reverse roles of hiding and finding pieces. Recite the verse together again.

PRAYER STATION

■ *Objective: Children will explore and practice prayer for themselves in small groups.*
■ *Materials: Copies of* StationMaster Card #9 *for each adult or teen helper*

Break into small groups of three to five children. Assign a teen or adult helper to each small group and give each helper a copy of *StationMaster Card #9* (see Resources, 97) with ideas for group discussion and prayer.

SNACK STOP: PUDDING TRUMPETS

If you plan to provide a snack, this is an ideal time to serve it.

■ *Materials: ice cream cones, pudding, plastic spoons*

Fill a cone with pudding and give one to each child with a spoon. Explain how the cones look like trumpets which are often used to announce something exciting that is about to happen. Let children eat their pudding and then "toot" their cones like trumpets before eating them. Talk about exciting events they have had or look forward to.

Note: Be aware that some children may have milk allergies and be prepared with another option if necessary.

APPLICATION

■ *Objective: Children will have opportunities to show how the lesson works in their own lives through activities and take-home papers.*

Some children's ministries may allow children to play outside at this point. If yours does not, choose one of the following activities.

Jump Alive!

Remind children that God is with them when they are excited. To help remember this, instruct kids to jump into the air and say, "That is awesome, God!" Practice this a few times. Explain that you will read a list. If you read something the children find exciting, they should jump into the air and shout, "That is awesome, God!" If they do not find the item exciting, they should stay seated. Not every child will jump every time, but that's okay. Then read the following list:

Birthdays, Christmas, tying your shoes, reading a book, sleeping, amusement parks, picnics, singing, laughing, surprises, presents, a new dog, praying, going to school, coming home from school, playing sports, making a home run, making the winning point in a game, playing board games, winning a board game, writing a letter, watching TV, playing a video game, playing an instrument, running, having a day off from school, getting sick, doing chores, going to the moon, riding on an airplane, taking off your shoes, going to the park, going to church, spending the night over at a friend's house, and cleaning your room.

At the end, if children have thought up ideas of things that are exciting, let them say them and have the class react to those ideas.

Praise Banners

- **Materials:** *card stock or poster board banners, glitter glue, markers or crayons, crepe paper, scissors, thin dowels, wide tape*

Give each child a "banner." Have students write "Praise God!" or another short statement of praise to God that would celebrate an exciting event. Then they will decorate their banners with glitter glue, art designs, and, if they choose, attach crepe paper streamers. Helpers can help fasten a dowel stick to the short side of the banner. If children complete their banners, lead them in a praise song, or let them chant their memory verse as they wave their banners.

ON THE FAST TRACK! *(Take-Home Papers)*

(Optional) As you hand out *On the Fast Track!* take-home papers, remind students they can delve into the treasure box if they complete the paper. **I'm giving everyone an *On the Fast Track!* paper to take home. To earn a prize from the treasure box, you must complete all the activities at home and learn your verse. When you're finished, ask your parents or guardian to sign the ticket and bring it next week. If you do, you'll get to choose a prize!**

Distribute the take-home papers just before children leave.

Memory Verse:

On my bed I remember you; I think of you through the watches of the night. **Because you are my help, I sing in the shadow of your wings** (Psalms 63:6–7).
Note: Younger children may memorize the shorter version of this verse in bold print.

Bible Basis:
Book of Job

Bible Truth:
God is there even when we are sick.

You Will Need:

- [ ] treasure map mounted on a wall
- [ ] construction paper in assorted colors
- [ ] zip-bag filled with real coins
- [ ] big pile of plush animals
- [ ] 30" length of yarn
- [ ] building blocks
- [ ] red adhesive dots
- [ ] roll of bathroom tissue
- [ ] paper child pattern (see Resources, 90)
- [ ] treat jar
- [ ] *Use the Clues!* poster with map clues
- [ ] *On the Fast Track!* #10 take-home paper
- [ ] *StationMaster Card #10*
- [ ] *(Optional)* treasure box
- [ ] *(Optional)* Snack: gelatin dessert squares, spoons, paper cups
- [ ] *(Optional)* Activity #1: cardstock, colored pencils
- [ ] *(Optional)* Activity #2: masking tape, large towel or cloth, pillow or rolled up shirt or coat, large bowl, plastic spoons, cereal o's.

 When you see this icon, it means preparation will take more than five minutes.

GET SET!
(Lesson Preparation)

- ■ Make a copy of *On the Fast Track #10* take-home paper for each child.
- ■ Make a copy of *StationMaster Card #10* for each helper.
- ■ ⊛ Make 10 copies of the child pattern (see Resources, 90) and cut them out. Hole punch the pictures at the top and color them if you wish. String 10 paper "children" on a 30" length of yarn and knot the ends together.
- ■ Set out the treat jar and *(optional)* treasure box.
- ■ Set up snack or outside play activities if you include these items in your children's ministry.
- ■ Mark two taped X's on the floor for optional Activity #2, if using.

TICKETS PLEASE!
(Welcome and Bible Connection)

- ■ *Objective: To excite children's interest and connect their own life experiences with the Bible Truth, children will create a sick room scene and talk about what is in their room when they're sick.*

Welcome Time Activity: Sick Room Set Up

- **Materials:** *construction paper in assorted colors, scissors, tape*
  Ask children who arrive early to create a sick room scene on a blank wall. They can draw big pictures of things that would be useful or common in their room when they're sick, cut them out, and arrange them on the wall with tape. Possible images: bed, pillows, pitcher and cup for juice, thermometer, medicine, favorite stuffed toy, vaporizer, chicken noodle soup, etc. Ask then what else is part of a sick room? Is God found there?

When everyone has arrived, welcome the children and offer them a treat from the *treat jar.* Say: **I'm so glad you are here again today to search for God. God likes it too when children search for Him. Whenever they do, He rewards them with His presence. The treats remind us of that reward.** Children may eat their treat now or take it home.

Sharing Time and Bible Connection

Introduce today's lesson by discussing the following questions. As you talk, give every child an opportunity to respond.

- **What kinds of things make people sick?** (flu, colds, germs, animal bites, bad food)
- **Who takes care of you when you're sick?**
- **What did you need to get better the last time you were sick?** (medicine, rest, God's healing)

Being sick is no fun. It might seem fun when you get to eat gelatin or stay in bed. But being sick can be really unhappy. Some people have really serious sicknesses, or are sick for a long time. After awhile it's not much fun to stay in bed, alone, and miss the fun your friends or family are having. <u>Even when you're laying in bed, sick, and feeling yucky, God is with you</u>. If you remember God when you are sick, you can feel better. A man named Job had a terrible sickness. Let's find out what happened to him.

ALL ABOARD FOR BIBLE TRUTH   Book of Job
(Bible Discover and Learn Time)

- **Objective:** *Children will study the book of Job to understand that Job recognized God's presence when he was very sick.*
- **Materials:** *Use the Clues! poster with map clues, string of paper children, zip-bag full of coins, big pile of plush animals, building blocks, red adhesive dots, roll of bathroom tissue*

Before you begin the Bible story, build a house out of building blocks at the front of your lesson area. You will need to recruit a teen or adult helper to be "Job" for today's lesson. Ask the helper to stand at the front of the room by the block house. Hang the string of paper children around his or her neck. Surround the helper's feet with a big pile of stuffed animals.

Way back in Bible times, a man named Job had ten children and lots of possessions. He had herds of animals, a big house, many camels, and a lot of gold. Helper should proudly show class his necklace of children and gesture toward the plush animals. Helper should also jingle the bag of gold and pat the house with pride of ownership as they are mentioned. **Job was a rich man.**

Job knew God and trusted Him. God was proud of Job. Then Satan decided to try to get Job to stop trusting God. Satan went to God and said, "Job is faithful to you now. But if you took away some of Job's stuff, he will say bad things about you!"

God said, "You may take away his stuff. But you may not hurt Job." Satan did his worst. In one day, all of Job's children were killed in accidents. Ask a child to remove the paper necklace from Job. **Then all his riches were taken away.** Ask another volunteer to take away the coins, a second volunteer to remove the plush animals, and a third to crash down the house. **When sad things happen in your life, how do you feel?** Accept children's responses. **Job probably felt like that.** Job should look sad.

But Job said to God, "You blessed me with all those things, and you have every right to take them away. Praise God!" Satan's plan didn't work.

So Satan went to see God again. "Job isn't saying anything bad about You because he's healthy. Make him sick, and he'll be angry at You." God said, "Okay, you may make him sick, but you may not kill him."

Satan was really nasty to Job. He made painful sores come out from the soles of his feet to the top of his head. Ask a volunteer to put red adhesive dots on Job's arms. Let another child spend a minute wrapping Job up in bathroom tissue.

Job's wife wasn't loving. She told him, "God did this to you! Curse Him and die!" Ask a volunteer to stand up and shake her fist at Job.

Job told his wife, "You're talking crazy. We accept good things from God, so we need to also be willing to accept trouble."

Then some of Job's friends came to visit. But instead of trying to make him feel better, they asked him, "What did you do wrong for God to be so mad at you?"

One said, "God definitely doesn't like you or He wouldn't let you suffer so much!"

Job told them he had done nothing wrong. They didn't believe him. The third friend said, "You must be very wicked for God to treat you like this." Have entire class stand and turn their backs on Job.

Look at Job. How do you think he would feel? (bad, sad, alone, sick) **He's sick and his wife and friends are treating him badly.**

Job said, "Maybe it would have been better if I had never been born." I imagine Job felt terrible and alone.

Then God spoke, "Are you in charge of the world? Do you keep it running? Are you going to tell me that I did something wrong?"

Job heard God. He realized God was there even while he was sick. His attitude changed. He answered God, "You can do all things, and no plan of yours is ever wrong. I know I'm part of your plan." What a change for Job!

Then God healed Job. Take off the bathroom tissue and red spots. **Not only that, God gave him more children and even more goods. Twice as much as he had before!** Give Job back the coins and the animals.

Job was sicker than most of us will ever be, but he still talked to God. He found out that God cares about how we feel when we're sick and hurting. He knows how alone and unhappy we are when we are sick. But we can't change our attitude unless we pay attention to God. He's there with us, but we have to talk to Him and listen to Him.

Point to the treasure map. **We can find God even when we're sick** by talking to Him and listening to Him. He will raise us out of the Muck of Misery. **Which clue did we discover today?** Help children decide that today's lesson was about the "God is with us when we are sick" clue. Choose a child to take it off the *Use the Clues!* board and place it on the map.

Use the Clues!
(Bible Review)

Okay, let's see what you remember.

- **What made Job sick?** (Satan made him sick to try to get him to stop following God)
- **Why did Satan do this to Job?** (he wanted Job to stop trusting God, God allowed it as a test for Job)
- **How did Job make it through that time of sickness?** (he never stopped trusting God, he talked to God and listened when God talked to him)
- **What did God do for Job?** (made him well, gave him more children and new goods)

- **How do we find God when we're sick?** (pay attention to Him and know He's there, talk to Him, read the Bible, sing or listen to praise songs, pray)

No matter how sick you are or how bad you feel, God is there with you. He cares about how you're feeling. He gives you hope and comfort and promises to stay with you, just like He did with Job. It's so good to know we can find God even when we're sick.

At this point, go through *Use the Clues!* found in the *Resource* section of this book to help children remember the Bible Truth. Use the treasure map and clues to review ways they can search for and find God.

BIBLE MEMORY WAYPOINT

Psalms 63:6–7

(Scripture Memory)

◼ *Objective: Children will hide God's Word in their hearts for guidance, protection, and encouragement.*

Write this week's memory verse on the board. Then, read it pointing to each word:

On my bed I remember you; I think of you through the watches of the night. Because you are my help, I sing in the shadow of your wings (Psalm 63:6–7).

To help children memorize the Bible verse, review it several times. When children are familiar with the verse, erase two words and ask children to read it again. The next round, erase two more words and repeat. Continue this until children can say the verse with almost no help.

PRAYER STATION

◼ *Objective: Children will explore and practice prayer for themselves in small groups.*
◼ *Materials: Copies of* StationMaster Card #10 *for each adult or teen helper*

Break into small groups of three to five children. Assign a teen or adult helper to each small group and give each helper a copy of *StationMaster Card #10* (see Resources, 98) with ideas for group discussion and prayer.

SNACK STOP: COMFORT FOODS (Optional)

If you plan to provide a snack, this is an ideal time to serve it.

◼ *Materials: gelatin dessert squares, spoons, paper cups*

Serve each child a small cup of gelatin dessert squares and talk about what kinds of things the children eat when they're sick. Foods like pudding or gelatin feel good on a sore throat, popsicles are nice after getting your tonsils out, etc. *Note: Always be aware of children with food allergies and have another option on hand if necessary.*

APPLICATION

■ **Objective:** *Children will have opportunities to show how the lesson works in their own lives through activities and take-home papers.*

Some children's ministries may allow children to play outside at this point. If yours does not, choose one of the following activities.

 ## Get Well Cartoons

■ **Materials:** *card stock, pencils, colored pencils or markers*

No one needs friends like Job's when they're sick. God uses friends to give encouragement and support when we're sick. That's a way we can see God during a time of being sick. Try making a short comic strip that will encourage or make a friend laugh when they're sick.

Have children fold the card stock in half to make a greeting card and make their cartoon on the front, then they can write an uplifting message inside. Prompt them to use words that remind the sick friend that God is there during their sickness.

 ## Hale and Healthy Relay

■ **Materials:** *masking tape, large towel or cloth, pillow or rolled up shirt or coat, large bowl, plastic spoons, cereal o's*

Mark out a three-station relay that emphasizes how to stay healthy. Imagine a baseball diamond-shaped play area. Fill the bowl with cereal o's and set on a table or chair at first base. Where the second base will be, make a tape X. At the third base location, lay out the towel and pillow. Make a final tape X at the home plate location. Children will start from there, each holding a plastic spoon. One will run to the bowl, take a spoonful of cereal o's to chew and swallow completely before running to the taped X. There the child will do five jumping jacks, then run to the towel and pillow. The player lays down with his head on the pillow as if sleeping, pulling the towel over as a blanket. Then the child jumps up and runs back to the starting X, tagging the next player who starts the relay. See how long it takes for the entire class to complete the relay.

 ### ON THE FAST TRACK! *(Take-Home Papers)*

(Optional) **Who would like to choose a prize from the treasure box?** Anticipate excited responses. Show the *On the Fast Track!* take-home papers. **Here's your *On the Fast Track!* paper to take home. To earn a prize from the treasure box, complete all the activities at home and learn your verse. When you're finished, ask your parents or guardian to sign the ticket and bring it next week. If you do, you'll get to choose a prize from the treasure box!**
Distribute the take-home papers just before children leave.

Valley of Sorrow

Memory Verse:

Why are you downcast, O my soul? Why so disturbed within me? Put your hope in God (Psalms 42:5).

Bible Basis:

1 Kings 17:7–24

Bible Truth:

God is with us when we are sad.

You Will Need:

- ☐ treasure map mounted on a wall
- ☐ puppets
- ☐ 1 sheet of poster board
- ☐ Bible time dress-up box
- ☐ pottery jar
- ☐ bean bag or small plush toy
- ☐ treat jar
- ☐ *Use the Clues!* poster with map clues
- ☐ *On the Fast Track! #11* take-home paper
- ☐ *StationMaster Card #11*
- ☐ *(Optional)* treasure box
- ☐ *(Optional)* Snack: fresh bread, softened or whipped cream cheese, squeezable jelly, plastic knives, napkins
- ☐ *(Optional)* Activity #1: four large posters of the memory verse written in phrases, four balls
- ☐ *(Optional)* Activity #2: inflated balloons each holding a verse of comfort

When you see this icon, it means preparation will take more than five minutes.

GET SET!

(Lesson Preparation)

- ■ Make a copy of *On the Fast Track #11* take-home paper for each child.
- ■ Make a copy of *StationMaster Card #11* for each helper.
- ■ Set out the treat jar and *(optional)* treasure box.
- ■ Set up snack or outside play activities if you include these items in your children's ministry.
- ■ 🌐 Print this week's Bible memory verse on a poster board and hang it up in the room: **Why are you downcast, O my soul? Why so disturbed within me? Put your hope in God (Psalm 42:5).**
- ■ 🌐 If using Activity #1, write the verse in phrases (Why are you downcast, O my soul?/Why so disturbed within me?/Put your hope in God/Psalm 42:5) on four separate sheets of poster board.
- ■ 🌐 If using Activity #2, write out these verses with references and insert one verse in each balloon. You can have duplicates since different children will receive them. Use a kid-friendly Bible translation, such as the CEV: Psalms 46:1; 86:4; 86:5; 86:15; 89:2; 91:15; 94:14a; Isaiah 66:13a; and Hebrews 13:5b. Roll up each paper and insert in a balloon, then inflate and tie the balloon. Make enough for each child to have one.

TICKETS PLEASE!
(Welcome and Bible Connection)

■ **Objective:** *To excite children's interest and connect their own life experiences with the Bible Truth, children will use puppets to share their sad experiences.*

Welcome Time Activity: Puppet Sharing

■ **Materials:** *any and all puppets*

Lay the puppets out so children arriving early can choose one. Have two or more children use the puppets to tell each other about a sad experience they've had and how they felt. The children can use inventive voices to give their puppets more character.

When everyone has arrived, welcome the children and offer them a treat from the *treat jar.* Say: **I'm so glad you came today to learn more about our search for God. Let's celebrate by having a treat!** Children may eat their treat now or take it home.

(Optional) If children returned a signed Fast Track! ticket, they may choose a prize from the treasure box.

Sharing Time and Bible Connection

Introduce today's lesson by discussing the following questions together.
Make a sorrowful face.

■ **When someone looks like I just did, what would you think that person is feeling like?** (sad) **Show me your sad faces.** Look around to see children's faces and have them observe other students' expressions.

■ **What kinds of things would cause you to have that sad look?**

Our lives have sad times, even when we wish they wouldn't. We can feel sad when someone moves away or someone we love is in trouble. Sometimes we're sad because our family has a hard time, or you can't do something you have been looking forward to. The one good thing we can count on when a sad time comes is that God is there with us. <u>**We can still find God in our lives even when we're sad.**</u>

📖 ALL ABOARD FOR BIBLE TRUTH

1 Kings 17:7–24

(Bible Discover and Learn Time)

- ■ **Objective:** *Children will study 1 Kings 17:7–24 and see how a lonely lady found God was near her when she was very sad.*
- ■ **Materials:** *Bible time dress-up box, Use the Clues! poster with map clues, pottery jug*

How about some volunteers to act out the story as I tell it? Choose an Elijah, a widow, and a son. Let them choose appropriate items from the dress up box. Explain that they will silently do the actions and make the expressions that match the story as you tell it. **In Old Testament times, a prophet named Elijah talked to God and God talked to him. In this story he meets a widow. Who can tell me what a widow is?** (a woman whose husband has died)

This widow had a sad life. Point to the widow. **Not only was her husband dead, she only had a tiny bit of food left. It was just enough food for one more meal for herself and her son. After that, she knew they would starve and die.** Widow looks in her jug and shakes head sadly.

Open your Bible to the passage and leave it open in your lap while you tell the story. **In 1 Kings 17, we read that God told Elijah to find this lady because she would take care of him. Elijah obeyed. He went to her town and found her.** Elijah walks to the widow. **He asked her, "Would you bring me a drink of water in a jar?"**

While she was getting him the water, Elijah called, "And could I have a piece of bread too, please?" This widow had almost no food for herself and her son. How was she supposed to feed a stranger? Widow fetches water with the jug, but looks worried.

She told Elijah, "I don't have any bread, only a handful of flour in a jar and a little oil in a jug. I'm gathering a few sticks to make a meal for myself and my son to eat before we die." Widow shows empty hands.

Elijah said to her, "Don't be afraid. Go home, and make some bread for me. Then make bread for yourself and your son. For God has said that your jar of flour will not be used up and your jug of oil will not be empty until God causes it to rain." Elijah points to jug. **Wow, what a surprising message!**

The widow did what Elijah said. Widow makes bread. **Guess what happened? There was food for all three of them that day. And the next day. And the next. The jar of flour and the jug of oil didn't run out.** Everybody eats and drinks.

But then the widow had another reason to be sad. Her son got sick. Then he died! Son lies down on the floor, eyes shut. **The widow asked Elijah, "What is the matter with me? Did God send you to remind me of my sin and kill my son?"** Widow is crying.

Elijah laid the boy on his bed and prayed to God, "Please give this boy back his life, God." Elijah prays over the son. **The Lord heard Elijah's**

prayer. The boy came back to life! Elijah gave him back to his mother and said, **"Your son is alive!"** Son gets up and jumps for joy.

Then the woman said, **"Now I know you are a man of God and your words are true."**

Lead class in applause for the actors, who can sit down. **The widow lost her husband, food, and son. Was God still with her?** (yes) **He sent his servant Elijah to her. When she chose to share her last bit of food with Elijah, God blessed her so that she would never be hungry again. He also raised her son from the dead.**

When we're sad, like this lady, we should remember that God cares about us. <u>God is with us when we are sad</u>. God can show us He's with us in ways we don't expect.

Point to the treasure map. **Anytime you're sad, think of the widow and how she's an example that <u>God is with us when we are sad</u>. If we look and find God, we can climb through the Valley of Sorrow. Which clue did we discover today?** Help children decide that today's lesson was about the "God is with us when we are sad." clue. Choose a child to take it off the *Use the Clues!* board and place it on the map.

Use the Clues!
(Bible Review)

Use these discussion questions to check for understanding of today's lesson:

- **Why was the widow sad?** (her husband had died, she didn't have enough food to stay alive, and then her son died)
- **How did the widow find God in her sadness?** (God sent Elijah to be with her and help her)
- **In what ways did God show the widow His presence?** (He kept her flour jug and oil jug from running out, He brought her son back to life)
- **How can you and I find God when we're sad?** (look for ways He's helping us, pray)

At this point each week, follow the *Use the Clues!* found in the *Resource* section to help children review the Bible Truth and remember ways they can search for God. Review all weeks up to this week.

BIBLE MEMORY WAYPOINT   Psalms 42:5
(Scripture Memory)

- *Objective: Children will hide God's Word in their hearts for guidance, protection, and encouragement.*
- *Materials: bean bag or small plush toy*

Read this week's memory verse from the poster board, pointing to each word:

Why are you downcast, O my soul? Why so disturbed within me? Put your hope in God (Psalms 42:5).

Invite the children to join you saying the verse out loud several times until they are familiar with it. To help children memorize the verse, play a passing game. Have children sit on the floor in a circle. Hand a bean bag to one child. As you play the music, the children will pass the beanbag to the lap of the child to his left. With each pass, the child holding the beanbag says the next word in the verse. Try to keep a steady rhythm. Repeat the verse, and challenge kids to go a little faster with each repetition.

PRAYER STATION

- **Objective:** *Children will explore and practice prayer for themselves in small groups.*
- **Materials:** *Copies of* StationMaster Card #11 *for each adult or teen helper*

Break into groups of three to five children. Assign a teen or adult helper to each small group and give each helper a copy of *StationMaster Card #11* (see Resources, 98) with ideas for group discussion and prayer.

SNACK STOP: ELIJAH'S SNACK (Optional)

If you plan to provide a snack, this is an ideal time to serve it.

- **Materials:** *fresh bread, softened or whipped cream cheese, squeezable jelly, plastic knives, napkins*

Ask the children what food Elijah asked the widow for. Give each child a slice of bread. Each one can spread cream cheese on the bread and make a sad face or a happy face with the squeezable jelly to show that God is with us even in sad times.

Note: Always be aware of children with food allergies and have another option on hand if necessary.

 **APPLICATION**

■ **Objective:** *Children will have opportunities to show how the lesson works in their own lives through activities and take-home papers.*

Some children's ministries may allow children to play outside at this point. If yours does not, choose one of the following activities.

 ### Memory Verse Toss

■ **Materials:** *four large posters with memory verse written in phrases, four balls*

Divide the class into four groups. Spread out in the hall so each group has its own wall space. Hang the four sheets of poster board with the memory verse broken into phrases on the wall. Hand each group a ball. Each group's first player tosses the ball against the wall and says quickly, "Why are you downcast, O my soul?" and moves out of the way. The next person lets the ball bounce and then catches it. That child tosses it against the wall and says, "Why so disturbed within me?" The next person lets it bounce, catches it, then tosses it and says, "Put your hope in God." The fourth person lets it bounce, catches it, then tosses it and says, "Psalm 42:5." Keep going through the verse two or three times, rotating players as many times as needed.

Comfort Pop

■ **Materials:** *inflated balloons each holding a verse of comfort*

Unleash the balloons into the room. If you think children need to release lots of energy, have them hop, skip, shuffle, and move in other ways through the balloons until you give a signal. Then each child grabs one and sits on it to pop it. Inside they'll find a verse of comfort. Have children share their verse with two other children; helpers or older children can help younger ones read theirs. Ask children to tell where they might save their verses until a time of sadness comes to them or someone else and they want to read it again or share it.

 ON THE FAST TRACK! *(Take-Home Papers)*

(Optional) **Who would like to choose a prize from the treasure box?** Show the *On the Fast Track!* take-home papers. **Today I'm going to give you an *On the Fast Track!* paper. To earn a prize, you must complete the activities this week and learn your verse. Then ask your parents or guardian to sign the ticket and bring it next week. If you do, you'll get to choose a prize from the treasure box!**

Distribute the take-home papers just before children leave.

LESSON TWELVE: That's Not Fair!

Thorns of Unfairness

Memory Verse:
We live by faith, not by sight (2 Corinthians 5:7).

Bible Basis:
1 Samuel 1

Bible Truth:
We can find God even when things seem unfair.

You Will Need:

- [ ] treasure map mounted on wall
- [ ] scrap or recycled paper
- [ ] 2 big boxes
- [ ] treat jar
- [ ] *Use the Clues!* poster with map clues
- [ ] *On the Fast Track!* #12 take-home paper
- [ ] *StationMaster Card* #12
- [ ] *(Optional)* treasure box
- [ ] *(Optional)* Snack: commercial or home-made mini crackers or cookies, the kind with cheese or frosting in the center, napkins
- [ ] *(Optional)* Activity #1: masking tape.
- [ ] *(Optional)* Activity #2: four large sheets of paper of different colors, Bible memory verses on slips of paper, scissors, markers

When you see this icon, it means preparation will take more than five minutes.

GET SET!
(Lesson Preparation)

- ■ Write and copy a short note to families reminding children to bring their treasure maps from home to class next week.
- ■ Make a copy of *On the Fast Track #12* take-home paper for each child.
- ■ Make a copy of *StationMaster Card #12* for each helper.
- ■ Set out the treat jar and (optional) treasure box.
- ■ Set up snack or outside play activities if you include these items in your children's ministry.
- ■ Break up some of the crackers or cookies if using them for the snack; put them in a bag
- ■ Make a label for each box. One should read, "FAIR" and the other, "UNFAIR"
- ■ Create a 2–3 foot wide center aisle in your room with masking tape if using optional Activity #1.
- ■ Print out the Bible memory verses from the previous four lessons if using optional Activity #2 on separate slips of paper

TICKETS PLEASE!
(Welcome and Bible Connection)

- ■ **Objective:** *To excite children's interest and connect their own life experiences with the Bible Truth, children will draw pictures of fair and unfair things and talk about them.*

Welcome Time Activity: Fair, Unfair

■ *Materials:* *white or chalk boards, white board markers or chalk*
Ask children to draw one picture that shows something that is fair, and another that shows something unfair. Ask them to explain their drawings to the other children.

When everyone has arrived, welcome the children and offer them a treat from the treat jar. Say: **God likes it when children search for Him. Whenever they do, He rewards them with His presence. The treats remind us of that reward.** Children may eat their treat now or take it home.

(Optional) If children returned a signed Fast Track! ticket, they may choose a prize from the treasure box.

Sharing Time and Bible Connection

Introduce today's lesson with a brief skit. Ask two children to the front. Whisper an unfair situation to them (such as being blamed for something they didn't do) and ask them to act it out.

Do you know what these two actors were showing us? Is this something that is fair or unfair? (unfair) Thank the actors who can sit down. Discuss the topic with the students and give each one an opportunity to say something.

■ **What kind of unfair things have happened to you?**
■ **How do you know when something is fair or unfair?** (the decision has to do with what you think someone deserves or doesn't deserve)
■ **Where is God when something unfair happens to you?**

Most people want to be fair and have fair things happen to them. But lots of unfair things happen to us too. Today's Bible story is about a woman who had a lot of unfair things in her life. Will she find out that <u>we can find God even when things seem unfair</u>? Let's find out!

ALL ABOARD FOR BIBLE TRUTH   1 Samuel 1
(Bible Discover and Learn Time)

■ *Objective:* *Children will study 1 Samuel 1 and learn that Hannah's life was unfair, but she knew God was there with her.*
■ *Materials:* *recycled paper, 2 big boxes labeled "FAIR" and "UNFAIR," Use the Clues! poster with map clues*

Hand out paper and direct children to take six sheets each. They should wad up each paper as tight as they can to make six balls. Explain that during the story when they hear about something fair or unfair, they should toss one of their paper balls into either the "FAIR" or "UNFAIR" box at the front of the lesson area.

Open your Bible to 1 Samuel 1 and keep it open as you tell today's story. **In Bible times men sometimes had more than one wife at a time. The Bible tells us that a man named Elkanah had two wives, Hannah and Peninnah. In those days, a wife was seen as valuable only if she had some children. A wife who had no children felt ashamed and people were not kind to her. Peninnah had children, but Hannah had none. Was this fair or unfair?** Have the children toss a paper wad into the box.

Every year Elkanah, took his wives, Peninnah and Hannah, to the town of Shiloh to offer sacrifices to God. Even though Hannah had no children, Elkanah still loved her more than his other wife. So he made a bigger sacrifice for Hannah than for Peninnah. Was that fair or unfair? Children toss another wad.

Peninnah wasn't happy about that. And because Hannah had no children, Peninnah was mean to her all the time. What do you think about that? Children toss another wad.

Every year when Elkanah, Hannah, and Peninnah went to Shiloh, Elkanah treated Hannah better because he loved her more. Then Peninnah would be so mean to Hannah that Hannah would cry and not be able to eat. Was that fair or unfair? Children toss another wad.

Elkanah told Hannah that he loved her more than ten sons, but it didn't make Hannah feel better. How she wanted a child!

One day, when they were at the temple in Shiloh, Hannah started praying to God. Over and over she asked God for a child! She promised God that if He would give her a son, she would let that son serve God for all his life. While she prayed, the head priest saw her. Hannah was praying in her heart and her lips were moving, but she didn't say any words out loud. The head priest thought she was drunk! He asked her, "Why are you drunk before the Lord?" Was that fair or unfair? Children toss another wad.

Hannah explained that she was telling God how much she wanted a baby boy. Do you know what? By the next year, God did bless her with a son! She was so excited. She named him Samuel, which means, "Because I asked the Lord for him." God had plans for Samuel. God chose him to be one of Israel's greatest leaders. God was waiting for just the right time but to Hannah, life seemed so unfair.

Hannah showed us exactly what to do when we feel we've been treated unfairly. What was that? (she remembered God, she prayed) **Hannah never forgot that God was right there with her. She talked to God often and told Him what she felt. Like Hannah, we can give our hurt feelings to God, because when we search, <u>we can find God even when things seem unfair</u>. God has a big plan that we can't see. But we can find Him, and wait for Him to work the unfairness out His way.**

Point to the treasure map. **Sometimes life is unfair. When things are unfair, we need to tell God how we're feeling. Then we trust Him to act on our behalf at the perfect time. If we do that, we won't be pricked by the Thorns of Unfairness. Which clue did we discover today?** Help children decide that today's lesson was about the "We can find God even when things seem unfair" clue. Choose a child to take it off the *Use the Clues!* board and place it on the map.

Here is an important announcement! Next week, bring your home treasure maps to show the class. *Emphasize this strongly.* **Everyone who brings in their treasure map will receive a prize.**

Use the Clues!
(Bible Review)

Okay, let's see what you remember.

- **What are some of the unfair things that happened to Hannah?** (she had no children, Elkanah's other wife treated her meanly, the high priest accused her of being drunk)
- **What did Hannah do to deserve all this unfairness?** (nothing, her life wasn't unfair because of something she had done)
- **How did Hannah search for God?** (she prayed a lot, she kept waiting and trusting in God)
- **How can we find God when things are unfair for us?** (pray, talk to people who know and trust God, wait, look for signs of how God is working on our behalf)

Take some time now to follow *Use the Clues!* (see Resources, 84–89) to help children review the Bible Truth. Use the treasure map and clues to review with children all the places they will find God.

BIBLE MEMORY WAYPOINT   2 Corinthians 5:7
(Scripture Memory)

- **Objective:** *Children will hide God's Word in their hearts for guidance, protection, and encouragement.*

Read this week's memory verse from your Bible and then write it on the board. Point to each word as you read it:

We live by faith, not by sight (2 Corinthians 5:7).

To help children memorize the Bible verse, use a clapping rhythm in tune with the words.

We live clap, clap
By faith clap, clap
Not clap, clap
By sight. Clap, clap
Second Corinthians clap, clap
Five, seven clap, clap, clap

Repeat several times. You can substitute a foot stomp, or pat a friend's back, for the clap, if you choose.

PRAYER STATION

- ■ **Objective:** *Children will explore and practice prayer for themselves in small groups.*
- ■ **Materials:** *Copies of* StationMaster Card #12 *for each adult or teen helper*

Break into small groups of three to five children. Assign a teen or adult helper to each small group and give each helper a copy of *StationMaster Card #12* (see Resources, 99) with ideas for group discussion and prayer.

SNACK STOP: RANDOM CRACKERS (Optional)

If you plan to provide a snack, this is an ideal time to serve it.

- ■ **Materials:** *napkins, bag of commercial or home-made mini crackers or cookies (some with cheese spread or frosting in the middle, and some without). Break some crackers in piece.*

On each child's napkin, shake out a small quantity of the crackers randomly. Allow some children to have a few more than others. Ask children to sort them based on the whole ones, broken ones, and ones without filling. Each child will have a different assortment of whole, filled and broken ones. Talk about how life is sometimes unfair, like getting more broken or empty crackers than other kids.

Note: Always be aware of children with food allergies and have another option on hand if necessary.

APPLICATION

■ *Objective: Children will have opportunities to show how the lesson works in their own lives through activities and take-home papers.*

Some children's ministries may allow children to play outside at this point. If yours does not, choose one of the following activities.

 ### The Far Side

■ *Materials: masking tape*

Create a middle section that is two to three feet wide in the center of your play area, and tape lines to designate this space. To play, one child is "It" and stands inside the taped section. Other children stand at one end of the room, with the goal of running to the other side, staying inside the center aisle. "It" tries to tag as many runners as possible. When tagged, children sit down where they are and try to tag others running by them. The game ends when everyone has been tagged. Expect some cries of "unfair" during the game, a chance to remind children that life is unfair. Ask them where God is when life is unfair.

 ### Memory Verse Rehearse

■ *Materials: large sheets of paper in four colors, markers, Bible memory verses on slips of paper, scissors, markers*

Divide into four groups. Give each group one of the memory verses from the past four weeks' lessons and have them write it in big letters on a large sheet of paper. Then they should cut it up into six to eight pieces. Choose two groups to hide their pieces around the room or play area while the other groups wait in the hall or outside. Then the waiting groups should find the verse pieces and assemble the verses correctly. Each group assemble pieces of one color. Finally, have everyone read, then recite from memory, those verses. Reverse roles and repeat the game.

 ### ON THE FAST TRACK! *(Take-Home Papers)*

(Optional) Ask who would like a prize from the treasure box. As you hand out the *On the Fast Track!* papers, explain their use. **To earn a prize from the treasure box, complete the activities this week and learn your verse. When you are finished, ask your parents or guardian to sign the ticket on the front and bring it next week. If you do, you'll get to choose a prize from the treasure box!**

Distribute the take-home papers just before children leave. Send home a note to remind children to bring their treasure maps next week.

LESSON THIRTEEN: Found!

Treasure!

Memory Verse:
Oh LORD, you have searched me and you know me (Psalms 139:1).

Bible Basis:
Luke 15:3–10

Bible Truth:
God constantly searches for us.

You Will Need:

- [ ] treasure map mounted on a wall
- [ ] treasure chest picture (see Resources, 90)
- [ ] party decorations (crepe paper, confetti, balloons, poster board for signs)
- [ ] gold glitter glue
- [ ] index cards
- [ ] play dough
- [ ] treat jar
- [ ] *On the Fast Track! #13* take-home paper
- [ ] *StationMaster Card #13*
- [ ] *(Optional)* treasure box
- [ ] *(Optional)* Snack: cupcakes or cake, punch, napkins, cups
- [ ] *(Optional)* Activity #1: treasure map rewards, glue sticks, cupcakes or cake, punch, napkins, cups
- [ ] *(Optional)* Activity #2: buzzers, bells or bean bag, class treasure map, *Use the Clues!* (Resources, 84–89), prizes (optional)

 When you see this icon, it means preparation will take more than five minutes.

GET SET!
(Lesson Preparation)

- ■ Print this week's Bible memory verse on a white board:
  Oh LORD, you have searched me and you know me (Psalms 139:1).
- ■ If making play dough rather than using a commercial product, use the recipe we've included.
- ■ Copy a treasure chest emblem (see Resources, 90) for each child; color and decorate an extra one with gold glitter glue for the classroom treasure map .
- ■ Make a copy of *On the Fast Track #13* take-home paper for each child. Cut off the bottom half of the paper so you can hand out the treasure chest emblem during class.
- ■ Make a copy of *StationMaster Card #13* for each helper.
- ■ Set out the treat jar and *(optional)* treasure box.

Play Dough Recipe
- ■ *2 c. flour*
- ■ *1 c. salt*
- ■ *4 T. cream of tartar*
- ■ *1 pkg. unsweetened dry drink mix for scent and color*
- ■ *2 c. warm water*
- ■ *2 T. cooking oil*

Stir over medium heat until mixture pulls away from sides to form a ball. Store in airtight container. *(for 8 to 10 children)*

- Set up snack or outside play activities if you include these items in your children's ministry.
- If you choose not to have the children decorate the room during the Welcome Time Activity, you should do so before they arrive.

TICKETS PLEASE!
(Welcome and Bible Connection)

- **Objective:** *To excite children's interest and connect their own life experiences with the Bible Truth, children will decorate the room for a party to celebrate finding the treasure today.*

Welcome Time Activity: Party Decoration

- **Materials:** *party decorations, such as crepe paper, confetti, balloons, poster board, markers, tape, scissors*

    Ask children to decorate the room to celebrate both the end of the study and finding the treasure today. They can make streamers from crepe paper, inflate balloons, sprinkle confetti on the snack table, and make signs using poster board.

When everyone has arrived, welcome the children and offer them a treat from the treat jar. Say: **Today is the last day of our adventure. Let's celebrate today by having a treat!** Children may eat their treat now or take it home.

(Optional) If children returned a signed Fast Track! ticket, they may choose a prize from the treasure box.

Sharing Time and Bible Connection

Introduce today's lesson by discussing the following questions. As you talk, be sure each child has an opportunity to say something.

- **Have you ever played hide-and-seek with a young child?**
- **Did you hide in the hardest place possible?**
- **When a small child searches for you, do they really find you, or do you find them?**

Sometimes it might feel like we're playing hide-and-seek with God and we're like the young child. Over the last twelve weeks, we've talked about places where we search for and find God. But guess what?
There is an exciting surprise! *All the while we're trying to find God, He is actually looking for us!* <u>God constantly searches for us</u>. **He loves us so much that He will never let us leave Him. That truth is a treasure!**

ALL ABOARD FOR BIBLE TRUTH

Luke 15:3–10

(Bible Discover and Learn Time)

- ■ **Objective:** *Children will study Luke 15:3–10 to find out that God actually is searching for us when we're lost from Him.*
- ■ **Materials:** *play dough, large silver dollar or half dollar coin, gold-glittered treasure chest emblem*

Explain that you're going to tell the children two parables. After each one, they will mold an object from play dough that reminds them of the parable.

When Jesus was on earth, He told people parables. Parables are short stories that help us understand an idea God wants us to know. Today I'll tell you two parables that Jesus told. They're in the Bible, in the book of Luke. Open your Bible to the book of Luke and keep it open while you tell the story. **After each one, you'll have a short time to make something that reminds you of that parable.**

This first parable is about sheep. Once there was a shepherd who had 100 sheep. He loved each and every one of those sheep. They were very important to him, and he took the best care of them. One day, while the sheep were grazing in a mountain meadow, the shepherd decided to count them to be sure they were all there. Count slowly from 90 to 99 as you point to children. **Ninety-nine? A sheep was missing! The shepherd was so concerned about the missing one, he immediately started to search for it. He checked every boulder and bush, every gully and rockslide. He didn't stop looking until he found the one missing sheep. When he found it—whew! Was he glad! He put the sheep over his shoulders and carried it back to safety with the rest of the flock. When he got home, he called his friends and family to come over for a celebration. "Come celebrate with me," he told everyone. "I found my lost sheep!"**

The Bible says that whenever someone who's lost from God is found, all of heaven celebrates. God is so very delighted when He finds someone who has been lost from Him. Give children several minutes to mold something that reminds them of the parable. Let them share their creations with each other before telling the next parable.

Jesus told another parable in Luke 15 about a coin. Hold up a large coin. **Once, a woman had ten coins. That might not sound like a lot to you, but for this woman, these ten coins were very precious. They were made of silver. One day the woman was looking at her treasure of ten silver coins. She counted them.** Have children count with you. **There were only nine! She counted again. Nine! What happened to the tenth coin? The woman searched all over her house. She looked under things and inside things. She swept every corner and inch of the house. No coin! She shook every jar and lighted a lamp so she could see into the dark spots. She searched and searched until finally . . . there is was! She found the lost coin. Oh, what a relief!** Give a huge sigh of relief. **She was so delighted to find the one missing coin that she called her neighbors and friends to come over for a party. "Hoorah! I found my missing coin," she told them all.**

The one missing coin was so precious to the woman that she didn't stop

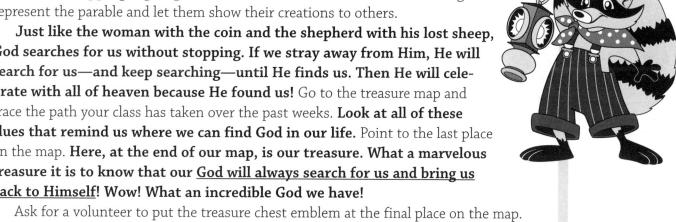

searching for it until she found it. **That's how God searches for us if we're away from Him. He loves us more than coins or sheep. And He searches for us without stopping.** Again give children a few minutes to create something to represent the parable and let them show their creations to others.

Just like the woman with the coin and the shepherd with his lost sheep, God searches for us without stopping. If we stray away from Him, He will search for us—and keep searching—until He finds us. Then He will celebrate with all of heaven because He found us! Go to the treasure map and trace the path your class has taken over the past weeks. **Look at all of these clues that remind us where we can find God in our life.** Point to the last place on the map. **Here, at the end of our map, is our treasure. What a marvelous treasure it is to know that our <u>God will always search for us and bring us back to Himself</u>! Wow! What an incredible God we have!**

Ask for a volunteer to put the treasure chest emblem at the final place on the map. Point to the treasure map. **We've traveled a long way on our search. And today we've found the treasure: <u>God constantly searches for us</u>!**

Use the Clues!
(Bible Review)

Use these questions to discuss today's lesson and check for understanding:

- **What is a parable?** (a short story Jesus told to help us understand something God wants us to know)
- **Why did the shepherd leave 99 of his sheep?** (to search for the lost one)
- **What happened when the woman lost one of her coins?** (she looked for it until she found it)
- **What did both the shepherd and woman do when they found the lost thing they had been searching for?** (they called everyone to come celebrate with them)
- **What do these parables mean?** (that God searches for each one of us who is away from Him and keeps searching until He finds us and we come back to Him)

Do the final review during the application time.

BIBLE MEMORY WAYPOINT
(Scripture Memory)

Psalms 139:1

- **Objective:** *Children will hide God's Word in their hearts for guidance, protection, and encouragement.*
- **Materials:** *index cards, markers, tape*

Read this week's memory verse from the white board. Point to each word as you read it:

Oh Lᴏʀᴅ, you have searched me and you know me (Psalms 139:1).

To help children memorize the Bible verse, have them divide into two groups (smaller classes can do this as a single group). Give groups 12 index cards, a marker, and tape. Have older children or a helper write one word of the verse on each of the cards. Then each child takes a card and tapes it to his chest. At your signal, the children arrange themselves so the verse is correctly spelled out. Then they recite it, first with each child saying his or her word, then in unison.

PRAYER STATION

- **Objective:** *Children will explore and practice prayer for themselves in small groups.*
- **Materials:** *Copies of* StationMaster Card #13 *for each adult or teen helper*

Break into small groups of three to five children. Assign a teen or adult helper to each small group and give each helper a copy of *StationMaster Card #13* (see Resources, 99) with ideas for group discussion and prayer.

SNACK STOP: PARTY FOODS

If you plan to provide a snack, integrate it this week with the Map Presentation and Party as suggested below.

- **Materials:** *cake or cupcakes, punch, napkins, cups*

APPLICATION

- **Objective:** *To celebrate with children not only their accomplishments as they've searched for God in every circumstance of life, but also their discovery of the great treasure of God's relentless pursuit of each precious child.*

Some children's ministries may allow children to play outside at this point. If yours does not, choose one of the following activities.

Map Presentations and Party

■ **Materials:** *children's treasure maps from home, treasure chest emblems (see Resources, 90), glue sticks, gold glitter glue, treasure map rewards, cupcakes or cake, punch, napkins, cups*

Have children who brought their treasure maps from home spread them out on tables or the floor. Distribute the final treasure chest emblem now, with instructions to decorate it with gold glitter glue and glue it to the end of the path. Encourage everyone to walk around and view the maps. Present a reward to each child who brought a map, even if the map is incomplete. Then have a class party to celebrate all that they've learned these thirteen weeks. Utilize the area decorated by the children in the Welcome Time Activity (or that you prepared). Serve cupcakes or cake and punch. Remind the children how heaven celebrates when someone is found by God and trusts in Jesus as their Lord and Savior.

Where Is God? Review

■ **Materials:** *buzzers or bells or bean bags, class treasure map, Use the Clues! (see Resources, 84–89), (optional) prizes*

Divide into two or more teams of at least four children per team. Set up a game show to have a fun and interactive review of all thirteen places on the map and what they represent. You can let children refer to the class treasure map during the game. If you believe children have memorized many of the weekly Bible verses, you can include them in the game also. If you have bells or buzzers for the number of teams you choose to have, you can use those. Otherwise, have the teams line up shoulder to shoulder in a circle or square with an object in the center. When you read a question, a child who knows the answer can run in to grab the object. That team then answers the question. If they're wrong, allow another team to answer. Make up questions using the *Use the Clues!* information and the Bible verses (optional). Play for a designated amount of time, or up to a predetermined number of points. You can award prizes if you choose.

ON THE FAST TRACK! *(Take-Home Papers)*

(Optional) **This is our last week for learning about where God is. Next week we'll start something new. But you can still bring back a signed ticket from this *On the Fast Track!* paper after you do the activities and memorize the verse. So take it home and do the work with your parents, then have them sign it so you can get a prize next week.**

Distribute the take-home papers just before children leave. Be sure they take home their treasure maps also.

Map Clue 1

When we search for God,

We will find Him.

We find God through the people in our family

Map Clue 2

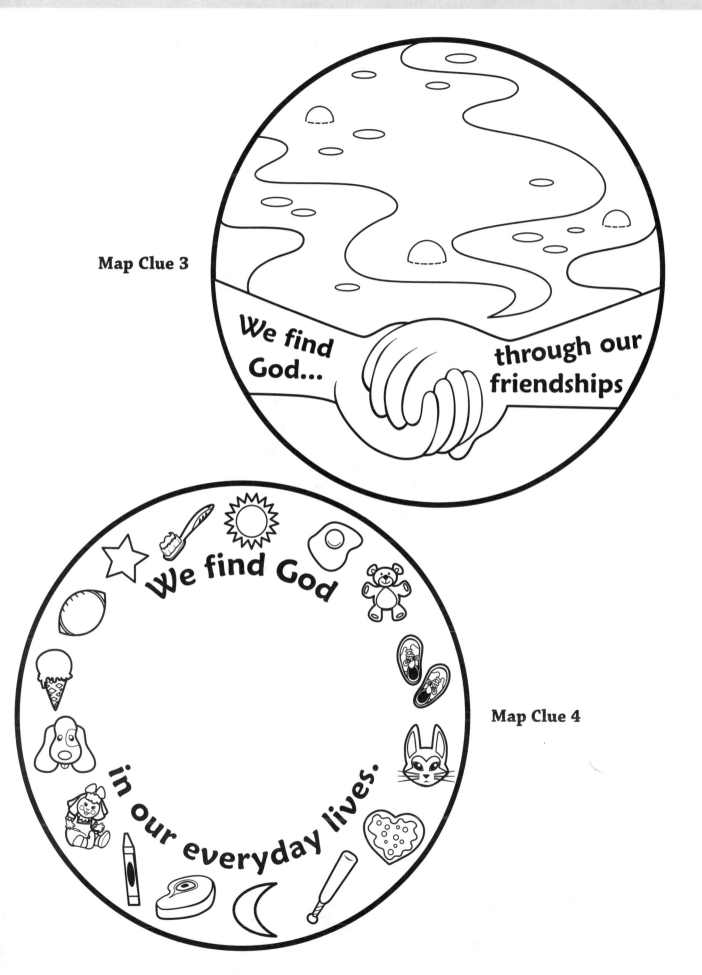

Map Clue 3

We find God... through our friendships

Map Clue 4

We find God in our everyday lives.

Map Clue 5

We find God in His awesome creation.

We find God at Church.

Map Clue 6

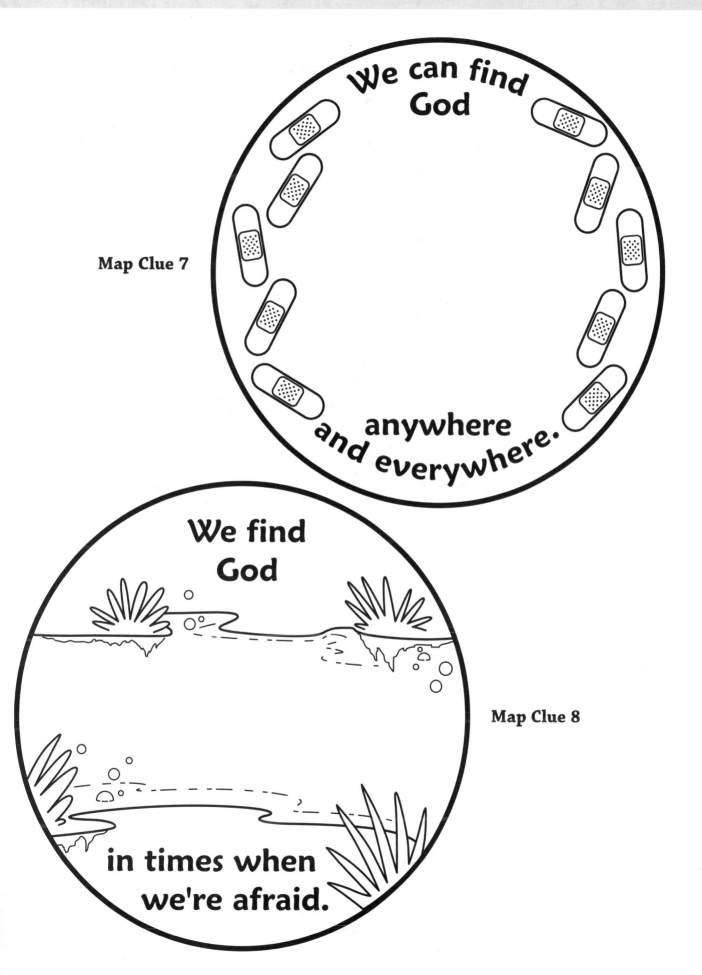

We can find God

Map Clue 7

anywhere and everywhere.

We find God

Map Clue 8

in times when we're afraid.

Map Clue 9

We find God in the middle of excitement.

God is there... even when we are sick.

Map Clue 10

Map Clue 11

God is with us when we are sad.

We can find God even when things seem unfair.

Map Clue 12

Map Clue 13

God constantly searches for us.

Bible Time Child

Treasure Map

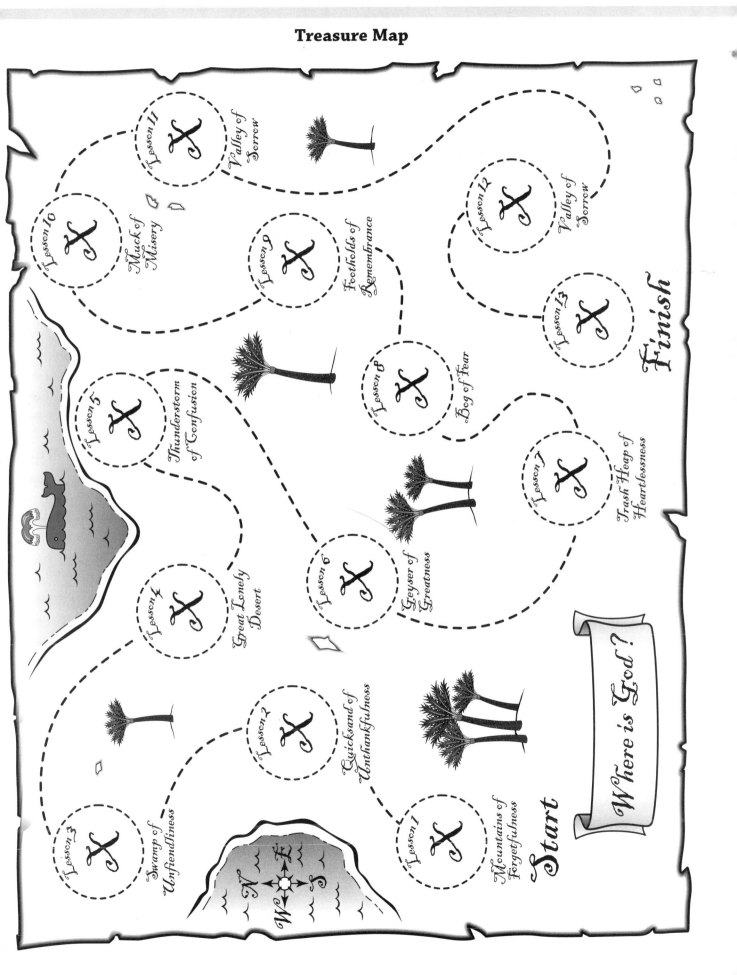

Dear Parents,

Where is God when we are sick? Can we see God in His handiwork? Where should we search for God and why? Over the next 13 weeks, our *Where Is God?* curriculum will challenge kids to explore the truth that God is present in every detail and circumstance of their lives through the theme of a treasure hunt–complete with a map and clues! What could be more fun?

After the first lesson, children will bring home a treasure map that they began in class. Your child might need a little extra help from you to finish the map and hang it on the wall in a good place. (A picture of the finished map is included in the first *On the Fast Track!* paper.) Kids will add a new clue to the map every week!

Every week, your child will receive an *On the Fast Track!* take-home paper with activities designed to reinforce the Bible truth for that lesson. Papers will include a Bible memory verse, a prayer challenge for parents and kids to do together, and a fun treasure map clue for kids to make. Encourage your child to complete these three activities and bring the signed *Fast Track!* ticket the following week for a prize.

Our small group prayer times will give children an opportunity to build lifetime habits of prayer. *Where Is God?* uses the **imPACT** model of prayer to help kids understand the four important activities of prayer—praise, ask, confess, and give thanks. Here are some discussion questions you can use at home to reinforce your child's growing desire to talk with God:

- *Praise.* Ask your child: **What do you really like about God? Listen to the responses. Let's tell God we like these things about Him.** Encourage your child to tell God about these things.

- *Ask.* It is important for children to know that God cares about their needs. Say: **We can ask God to help us, our families, and our friends with any problems. What would you like to ask God?** Let your child name some prayer requests, then take turns praying for these needs.

- *Confess.* Tell your child that we all do things we wish we didn't do. Sometimes our actions or words hurt someone and then we are sorry. Ask: **What's one thing you wish you didn't do this last week?** Listen to the response, then, together, bow heads and confess this sin before God.

- *Give thanks.* Ask: **What are some things that you're thankful that God has done for you or has given to you?** Listen to the responses. Then say: **Let's tell God thank you for these things.** Take turns thanking God.

If you have any questions about this study, please feel free to discuss them with the children's ministry leaders. We are excited about what God is going to do in the lives of our children. We would appreciate your prayers for the teachers and children.

In His Name,

Children's Ministry Coordinator

Dear Children's Ministry Helper,

Welcome to *Discipleship Junction!* During the next 13 weeks, you will play a major role in the lives of children as you teach them to look for God in every circumstance of life and pray with them in small groups. Our *Where Is God?* curriculum will help you build habits of prayer into their lives that will last a lifetime.

The **imPACT** model of prayer will remind children about the four important activities of prayer: praise, ask, confess, and give thanks:

- *Praise. Ask:* **What do you you really like about God?** Let volunteers briefly respond, then say: **Let's tell God we like these things about Him.** Help children talk to God directly.

- *Ask.* Ask children: **What would you like to ask God?** Allow children to give prayer requests, then say: **Let's tell God about these needs.** It is important for children to know that God cares about everyone's needs. Have them take turns praying for the needs in their lives.

- *Confess.* We all do things we wish we didn't do. Sometimes our actions or words hurt someone and then we are sorry. Ask them: **What's one thing that you wish you didn't do this last week?** Give children time to answer, then say: **Let's confess our sins to God and tell Him we're sorry.**

- *Give thanks.* When giving thanks, ask your group: **Tell one thing that you're thankful that God has done for you.** Let children share, then say: **Let's tell God thank you for these things.**

The children's ministry appreciates the important role that you have volunteered to fill. We are confident that God is going to do amazing things in the lives of our children.

Sincerely,

Children's Ministry Coordinator

StationMaster Card #1

This week children have discovered that <u>when we search for God, we will find Him.</u> The Bible passage comes from Jeremiah 29:13. Today, you'll lead your group in prayer according to the imPACT model (Praise, Ask, Confess, and Thanks). As your children engage in these four activities of prayer, focus their thoughts on today's lesson:

- *Praise.* **In our Bible passage today, we learned that we will always find God when we search for Him.** Have students praise God because He wants us to find Him.
- *Ask.* Students can ask God to remind them to seek Him this week.
- *Confess.* **Sometimes we forget God is with us.**

Let's ask him to forgive us for those times. Allow students to ask for forgiveness from God for times they forget God is there.

- *Thank.* **Never forget that God has promised that if you search for Him, you'll find Him.** Have students thank God for His patience. Remind them that they might forget God, but that He will never forget them. End your time of prayer by thanking Him for each child in your group.

Remember that no child should be forced to pray, but encouraged and invited to join you. After you have said, "Amen," talk quietly with your group until the next activity.

StationMaster Card #2

This week your group discovered that <u>God teaches us about Himself through our families</u>. The Bible passages we used are Exodus 20:12; Leviticus 19:3; Deuteronomy 1:31; Proverbs 1:8, 13:1, 15:5, 22:6; Isaiah 66:13; Mark 10:16; Ephesians 6:1–4; Colossians 3:20; 1 Thessalonians 2:7; Hebrews 12:7. Lead your group now in these four activities of prayer and help them focus their thoughts on today's lesson:

- *Praise.* **Today we found out that God gave us our families and each person in them. We learn about God through our families.** Have students praise God for something specific about their families.
- *Ask.* **Family members can show each other God's love.** Let students ask God to help them treat their family members well. They can be specific here also.
- *Confess.* **Our families aren't perfect, but God is.** Give students time to ask for forgiveness for not obeying their parents or being unkind to siblings.
- *Thank.* **Every family is different, but your family is the one God gave to you. How can you thank God for your family?** End your time of prayer by thanking Him for each child in your group.

Remember that no child should be forced to pray, but encouraged and invited to join you. After you have said, "Amen," talk quietly with your group until the next activity.

StationMaster Card #3

This week your group learned that <u>we can find God through our friendships</u>. The Bible passage is 1 Samuel 13—20. In today's prayer time, encourage your students to think about their friendships.

- *Praise.* **Today we learned from the Bible that Jonathan and David were really good friends.** Model for students how to praise God for being their true Best Friend. Remind students that human friends make mistakes, but God's friendship is never mean or unfair. His friendship is perfect.
- *Ask.* **God shows His love to people when they treat their friends well.** Give students opportunity to ask God to show them how to be a good friend. Encourage them to name those they want to be a good friend to.
- *Confess.* **God wants our friendships to be like David's and Jonathan's.** Have students confess times they've been mean or unfair to friends.
- *Thank.* **God can show His love through many different friendships.** Let children thank God for their friends. End your time of prayer by thanking Him for each child in your group.

Remember that no child should be forced to pray, but encouraged and invited to join you. After you have said, "Amen," quietly talk to the children until the next activity.

StationMaster Card #4

This week the children learned that <u>we find God in our every day lives</u> from Genesis 1:11–12, 24–25; Psalms 4:8; 23:1–4; 34:4; 40:1; 46:1; 84:11; 85:12; 147:8; 1 Timothy 4:4; and 2 Timothy 3:16. As you lead your children in the four activities of prayer, help them think about these things:

- ◼ *Praise.* **We learned today from the Bible that God is in every part of our lives from when we get up in the morning to when we go to sleep at night.** Students can praise God for being involved in our lives and able to be with everyone, everywhere.
- ◼ *Ask.* **Because God doesn't make us ask Him for every breath of air or drop of water that we need, sometimes we forget He's there.** Have students ask God to show them what He has done and is doing in their lives.

- ◼ *Confess.* **Do you sometimes forget that God has given you all you have, and stays with you every day?** Allow students to tell God they're sorry for not acknowledging what He does for them, and giving Him credit for all the good things in their lives.
- ◼ *Thank.* **When we're alone, it's especially good to know God is there.** Have students thank God for letting them find that He is active in their lives. End your time of prayer by thanking Him for each child in your group by name.

Remember that no child should be forced to pray, but encouraged and invited to join you. After you have said, "Amen," quietly talk to the children until the next activity.

StationMaster Card #5

Today, your group learned that <u>we can find God in His awesome creation</u>. The Bible passage we looked at is Genesis 1:11–14. Take some time now to help your students think about the world they live in and its amazing Creator.

- ◼ *Praise.* **In Genesis we learned that God created plants, trees, days, and nights— everything! What about creation do you want to praise God for today?** Encourage them to praise Him for the details He puts in all natural things from the smallest blade of grass to the biggest mountain.
- ◼ *Ask.* **God's handiwork is spectacular. We see His majesty in it.** Model for students how to ask God to show them Himself in nature.

- ◼ *Confess.* **God made nature, so we should praise Him, the Creator, and not the things He created.** Give time for students to apologize to God if they've ignored Him by focusing on created things instead.
- ◼ *Thank.* **If God's creations amaze us, just think how amazing God must be.** Go around the group, allowing students to thank God for showing them His fingerprint in nature. End your time of prayer by thanking Him for each child in your group by name.

Remember that no child should be forced to pray, but encouraged and invited to join you. After you have said, "Amen," quietly talk to the children until the next activity.

StationMaster Card #6

This week the children have learned that <u>we find God at church</u>. The Bible passage comes from Psalm 51:15–17. Take some time now to lead your group in prayer according to the imPACT model (Praise, Ask, Confess, and Thanks). As your children engage in these four activities of prayer, you can further focus their thoughts on today's lesson:

■ *Praise.* **Today we found out from the Bible that God is wherever His followers gather. Let's praise God that He is at church.** Ask what they can praise God for about their church, then give them time to praise God in prayer.

■ *Ask.* **In what ways do we see God in church with us?** Give children opportunity to recall what kind of attitudes and actions in church best show God's character through us. Then they can ask God to teach them these attitudes and actions.

■ *Confess.* **God delights in a broken and contrite heart. That means He's glad when we are sorry for the wrong things we've done.** Provide time for children to ask forgiveness for a time at church when they've chosen to exalt themselves instead of Him.

■ *Thank.* **God wants us to enjoy Him during our church worship time.** Have students thank God for being in their worship time. Encourage them to thank Him for specific aspects of worship where they feel most likely to see or sense God's presence. End your time of prayer by thanking Him for each child in your group by name.

Remember that no child should be forced to pray, but encouraged and invited to join you. After you have said, "Amen," quietly talk to the children until the next activity.

StationMaster Card #7

Today the children learned from Luke 10:30–37 that <u>we can find God working anywhere and everywhere in the world</u>. When God lives in us we will help and care for others the way God does. Take some time now to pray with your children and help them think about ways they can act in kindness toward others.

■ *Praise.* **Today from the Bible we learned how God used a Samaritan to show kindness to a hurt man.** Give students a chance to praise God for how He uses His followers to help others.

■ *Ask.* **We need to care for others, too. What shall we ask God about that?** If they're uncertain, prompt children to ask God to help them to act in love and kindness toward others.

■ *Confess.* **Can you think of a time when you could have helped someone or shown kindness but you did not?** Give children an opportunity to ask God to forgive them for these instances.

■ Thank. **God shows His kindness through other people all over the world.** Children can thank God that people in other countries can find God, just like they can. They might also want to thank God for wanting to be found by us.

Remember that no child should be forced to pray, but encouraged and invited to join you. After you have said, "Amen," quietly talk to the children until the next activity.

StationMaster Card #8

This week the children studied 1 Kings 19:1–18 to learn how <u>we find God in times when we're afraid</u>. As you lead your children in the four activities of prayer, help them think about looking for God when they are afraid.

- *Praise.* **Elijah was scared in the Bible story. But God reminded Elijah that He was there. He's with you, too.** Students can praise God for ways they've found God this past week.
- *Ask.* **Elijah was afraid of Queen Jezebel. He should have asked God for help instead of running away. What would you like to ask God about things that scare you?**

- *Confess.* **Like Elijah, we make the mistake of letting our fear get hold of us, instead of looking for evidence of God. This is a chance for you to ask God's forgiveness for the times you've done that.**
- *Thank.* **God always shows Himself to us in some way when we look for Him.** Have students thank God for being found anytime we look for Him.

Remember that no child should be forced to pray, but encouraged and invited to join you. After you have said, "Amen," quietly talk to the children until the next activity.

StationMaster Card #9

Today the children discovered that <u>we find God in the middle of our excitement</u>. The Bible passages were 2 Samuel 22 and Psalm 150. You will now lead your group in prayer according to the imPACT model (Praise, Ask, Confess, and Thanks). As your children engage in these four activities of prayer, you can further focus their thoughts on today's lesson:

- *Praise.* **One way to include God in our excitement is to praise Him for it.** Encourage students to praise God for being the Creator of all good things. They can specifically praise Him in relation to a recent exciting time.
- *Ask.* **When something exciting happens, we can forget God because we're so excited.** Students can ask God to remind them that He is in the middle of their exciting moments and

remember to give Him the place of honor when life gets exciting.

- *Confess.* **What should you do when you realize you've left God out of an exciting event?** Students ask God to forgive them for being too busy to notice Him when life gets exciting.
- *Thank.* **In our Bible passage today, we learned that God gives us our exciting times. Right now you can thank our Father in heaven for giving you those special times, like birthdays or vacations or getting a new puppy.** Allow children to thank God as they choose.

Remember that no child should be forced to pray, but encouraged and invited to join you. After you have said, "Amen," quietly talk to the children until the next activity.

StationMaster Card #10

This week your group heard a lesson from the book of Job and learned <u>that God is there even when we are sick</u>. As you pray with your children, help them understand that God's promise of comfort and hope in sick times applies to them, just like Job.

■ *Praise.* **In our Bible passage today, we learned that God is in charge of everything, even our sickness and health.** Allow children to praise God that He is in control of all our circumstances. Prompt them to choose a situation for which they can praise Him.

■ *Ask.* **Job got really sick.** Children who have sick friends or family can ask God for healing, comfort, and encouragement for these sick ones.

■ *Confess.* Remind the students how easy it is to feel miserable and complain when we are sick. Help children ask God's forgiveness for times they've had a complaining spirit.

■ *Thank.* **God answered Job. Has God answered one of your prayers recently? This is a chance to thank Him.** Students can thank God for whatever they choose. End your time of prayer by thanking Him for each child in your group.

Remember that no child should be forced to pray, but encouraged and invited to join you. After you have said, "Amen," quietly talk to the children until the next activity.

StationMaster Card #11

Today your group learned that <u>God is with us when we are sad</u>. The Bible passage was 1 Kings 17:7–24. As you lead your group in these four activities of prayer, help them remember that God cares deeply for every detail of their lives. He is with them when they are sad.

■ *Praise.* **In our Bible story, we saw how God helped a widow who had many sad times.** Have students praise God for knowing what's going on at all times in their lives.

■ *Ask.* **Elijah talked to God, so he knew what to do even in sad times.** Allow children to ask God to help them and show them His presence when they are sad. Have children pray for people they know are having sad experiences right now.

■ *Confess.* **God is waiting to comfort those who pray to Him.** Give students time to confess any wrongs they've committed.

■ *Thank.* **When someone is sad we don't always know what to say or do. But God knows exactly how to comfort us and show us He's there with us.** Have students thank God for always being there to comfort them. End your time of prayer by thanking Him for each child in your group.

Remember that no child should be forced to pray, but encouraged and invited to join you. After you have said, "Amen," quietly talk to the children until the next activity.

StationMaster Card #12

This week the children realized that <u>we can find God even when things seem unfair</u>. The Bible passage comes from 1 Samuel 1. Please lead your group in prayer according to the imPACT model (Praise, Ask, Confess, and Thanks). As your children engage in these four activities of prayer, help them focus on the truth that God's plan for their lives is perfect and can be trusted.

- *Praise.* **In our Bible story today, we learned God had a plan for Hannah.** Allow students to praise God for being in charge and having a perfect plan for their lives.
- *Ask.* **You can ask God to remind you He's there when you're upset or tempted to complain because things don't seem fair.**

Let's do that right now.
- *Confess.* **Instead of complaining, Hannah went to God and told Him all her problems. If you know you've complained about something that's unfair, you can ask God to forgive you.**
- *Thank.* Let children choose how they want to thank God. If they can't think of anything, suggest they thank Him for His perfect plan for their lives. End your time of prayer by thanking Him for each child in your group by name.

Remember that no child should be forced to pray, but encouraged and invited to join you. After you have said, "Amen," quietly talk to the children until the next activity.

StationMaster Card #13

Treasure found! This week the children learned an amazing truth: All the while we're trying to find God, He is actually looking for us! Your group studied Luke 15:3–10 to find that <u>God constantly searches for us</u>. As your children engage in these four activities of prayer, you can further focus their thoughts on today's lesson:

- *Praise.* **In our Bible story today, we learned that God constantly searches for us.** Have students praise God that He has such a huge love for them that He keeps searching for them until they come to Him.
- *Ask.* **When God searches for us, we all want to be found, don't we?** Encourage the children to ask God to keep them close to Him.

- *Confess.* **We all do things we wish we didn't do.** Give kids a minute of silence to think of something from this past week. Then invite them to ask God's forgiveness for it.
- *Thank.* **The treasure we discovered is that God keeps searching for us and rejoices when we give our lives to Him. Let's thank God for constantly searching for us.** Lead the children in a prayer of thanksgiving, giving each a chance to pray as they desire. End your time of prayer by thanking Him for each child in your group by name.

Remember that no child should be forced to pray, but encouraged and invited to join you. After you have said, "Amen," quietly talk to the children until the next activity.

On the Fast Track!

Dear Parents:

For thirteen weeks, our children's ministry will search for God together. Today children learned from Jeremiah 29:13 that <u>when we search for God, we will find Him</u>.

This week you can reinforce the lesson by talking together about how God might show His presence when your child is alone. End your time together praying as your child prayed in class, encouraging your child to add his or her own prayers to each section.

■ *Praise* God because He wants us to find Him.

Prayer Challenge

■ *Ask* God for reminders to seek Him this week.
■ *Confess* and ask God's forgiveness for times you forgot God was with you.
■ *Thank* God that even when we might forget Him, He never forgets us.

Your child may be shy at first and not want to add to the prayers out loud, but as you pray each week he or she will become more comfortable. If you have questions, feel free to discuss them with someone in the children's ministry program. We're excited about what God is doing and appreciate your prayers for the teachers and children in the weeks to come.

Bible Memory Verse

You will seek me and find me when you seek me with all your heart (Jeremiah 29:13).

Congratulations! You're starting an incredible journey to find God. Your home treasure map will help you remember what you learn each week. This week, complete the map that you started in class. Make it look like the map in the picture.

Ask your parents where you can hang your map at home. Each week you will make a clue to add to your map. Bring your map back on the last day of class for a prize!

Remember to climb over the Mountains of Forgetfulness as you search for God every day. To help you remember, color and cut out the clue (the circle to the right). Make your clue cool by gluing some macaroni on the mountains. Then glue the clue over the #1 on your treasure map.

When we search for God, We will find Him.

Dear Parents and Guardians,

Please check off the items your child completed this week:

❑ Prayer Challenge
❑ Map Clue
❑ Memory Verse

Adult Signature: _____

FAST TRACK! TICKET

On the Fast Track!

Dear Parents:

Today your child learned that <u>we find God through the people in our families</u>. Our Bible passages were Exodus 20:12; Leviticus 19:3; Deuteronomy 1:31; Proverbs 1:8, 13:1, 15:5, 22:6; Isaiah 66:13; Mark 10:16; Ephesians 6:1–4; Colossians 3:20; 1 Thessalonians 2:7; Hebrews 12:7.

This week talk with your child about times you've seen God's love through your family: kids sharing toys, Mom and Dad being patient, everyone speaking in kind voices, etc. Also talk about times when you haven't seen God's love: when people are arguing, when someone is impatient or unkind.

Prayer Challenge

End this time together as the children prayed in class. Encourage your child to add his or her own prayers to each section.

- ■ **Praise** God for your family.
- ■ **Ask** God for help to treat family members kindly.
- ■ **Confess** times of disobedience, unkindness, or selfishness.
- ■ **Thank** the Lord for showing His love through your family.

As you pray regularly together, your child will become more comfortable praying out loud with you. If you have any questions, please feel free to discuss them with anyone in the children's ministry program.

Bible Memory Verse

Give thanks in all circumstances, for this is God's will for you in Christ Jesus (1 Thessalonians 5:18).

Well done! You found clue 2 in your search for God. Quicksand is mushy, wet sand. If you struggle with quicksand, you will sink down into it. Bitterness or envy is just like quicksand. Being thankful that your family keeps you on solid ground. You won't get stuck in the Quicksand of Unthankfulness!

Color and cut out the clue to the right. Spread some glue on the solid ground and sprinkle sand over the glue. Tap the extra sand off outside. After it dries, glue it over #2 on your treasure map.

We find God through the people in our family

Dear Parents and Guardians,
Please check off the items your child completed this week:

- ❑ Prayer Challenge
- ❑ Map Clue
- ❑ Memory Verse

Adult Signature: _____

FAST TRACK! TICKET

On the Fast Track!

Dear Parents:

Today your child learned from 1 Samuel 13—20 that <u>we find God through our friendships</u>. Discuss friendship with your child. Tell about a good friend you've had. Then share about someone you thought was a friend until that person did not show God's love to you. Ask your child for an example of a friend who has shown God's love. End this time together by praying together using the guide below and encouraging your child to add his or her own prayer thoughts.

Prayer Challenge

- ■ *Praise* God for being a true Friend who never hurts us or lets us down.
- ■ *Ask* God to show your child how to be a good friend to others.
- ■ *Confess* times he or she has been mean, unloving, or unfair to friends.
- ■ *Thank* God for all the friends He's given.

As you pray regularly together every week, your child will become more comfortable praying out loud. If you have any questions, please discuss them with members of the children's ministry team.

Bible Memory Verse

A friend loves at all times (Proverbs 17:17).

Way to go! You discovered clue 3 in your search for God. This week we talked about trekking through the Swamp of Unfriendliness. A swamp is a marshy, wet area where alligators, lizards, and snakes live. Shallow water covers the land. Swamps can be dangerous if you don't have a boat to paddle through it. Being a friend is like a paddle that gets you through the Swamp of Unfriendliness.

Color and cut out the clue to the right. Make it better by mixing three colors of paint or markers that look dark and murky when they are combined. Color the swirls on your clue a dark, swampy color. Write your name on one hand, and the name of a friend on the other. Then glue it over #3 on your treasure map.

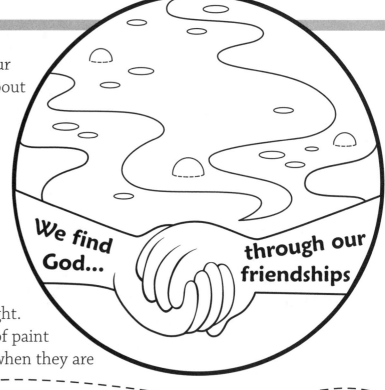

We find God... through our friendships

Dear Parents and Guardians,

Please check off the items your child completed this week:

- ❑ Prayer Challenge
- ❑ Map Clue
- ❑ Memory Verse

Adult Signature: _____

FAST TRACK! TICKET

On the Fast Track!

Prayer Challenge

Dear Parents:

Today, our children learned that we find God in our everyday lives. Our Bible passages were Genesis 1:11–12, 24–25; Psalms 4:8; 23:1–4; 34:4; 40:1; 46:1; 84:11; 85:12; 147:8; 1 Timothy 4:4; and 2 Timothy 3:16.

Talk with your child about times they've seen God in their lives. Share an example of when you have seen God working in your life. Look up these verses together: Psalms 40:5; 46:1; and 37:23–24. You can even memorize one as a family. Close this time by praying out loud together:

■ **Praise** God for being involved in our lives and that He's able to be with everyone, everywhere.

■ **Ask** God to show your child what He is doing in his or her life.
■ **Confess** times we haven't given God credit for all good things He does for us.
■ **Thank** God for one specific way your child sees God involved in his or her life.

As you pray together each week, your child will become more comfortable praying out loud. If you have any questions, please discuss them with a children's ministry leader.

IMPORTANT: Next week our class needs "clean trash" for a project. Please send empty cereal and food boxes, washed plastic containers, and recyclable paper to class with your child. Thank you!

Bible Memory Verse

God has said, "Never will I leave you; never will I forsake you" (Hebrews 13:5b).

You're doing it! You found clue 4 in your search for God. This week, we figured out how to avoid the Great Lonely Desert. We learned that we can always see God in the world around us, and even when we feel like we're all alone, God is right there with us.

Cut out the clue to the right. Before coloring it, draw something that reminds you that God never leaves you, like a star, a heart, a cross, or your own idea. Trace the shape with glitter glue and let it dry. Then color the rest of the clue and glue it over #4 on your treasure map.

Now when you look at your treasure map this week, thank God for being with you every day in every way! Remember that if you bring your map to class on _____ , you'll win a prize!

We find God in our everyday lives.

Dear Parents and Guardians,

Please check off the items your child completed this week:

❑ Prayer Challenge
❑ Map Clue
❑ Memory Verse

Adult Signature: _____

FAST TRACK! TICKET

On the Fast Track!

Dear Parents:

Today our children learned that <u>we find God in His awesome creation</u>. Our Bible passage was Genesis 1:11–14. This week take your child for a walk around your neighborhood. Point out God's creativity in everything from blades of grass to distant mountains or plains. You can even lie on your backs and marvel at the designs God makes in the clouds. Finish this time by praying together:

■ **Praise** God for the parts of creation you've seen and experienced today.

Prayer Challenge

■ **Ask** God to show you His wonderful character in nature.
■ **Confess** a time when you appreciated God's creation more than you appreciated God, who made it.
■ **Thank** God for leaving His fingerprint in nature to show us how awesome He is.

As you pray together every week, your child will become more comfortable praying out loud. If you have any questions, please discuss them with our children's ministry leaders.

Bible Memory Verse

Sing to the LORD, all the earth; proclaim his salvation day after day (1 Chronicles 16:23).

Isn't God amazing? You have found clue 5 in your search for God. This week, you learned to protect yourself from the Thunderstorm of Confusion! When you praise God, the Creator of all nature, instead of praising the things He made, you will be safe in stormy times.

Have you seen a thunderstorm? Electricity crackles and thunder booms! There may be dark clouds and soaking rain. Wild weather can be confusing and even a little scary. But don't forget! Our awesome Creator God is in charge of every storm.

Color and cut out clue 5. Make it cool by adding cotton balls to the cloud shapes. Cut out a lightning bolt from aluminum foil. Glue these to the clue, then glue the clue over #5 on your treasure map. Remember: bring your map to class on _____ (space for date to be included) to receive a reward.

We find God in His awesome creation.

Dear Parents and Guardians,

Please check off the items your child completed this week:

❑ Prayer Challenge
❑ Map Clue
❑ Memory Verse

Adult Signature: _____

FAST TRACK! TICKET

On the Fast Track!

Prayer Challenge

Dear Parents:

Today our children learned that we find God at church. Our Bible passage was Psalm 51:15–17. This week talk with your child about your church worship service. Ask how he or she is aware of God in church. Praise God for showing His presence in church. Pray together using the following outline and encourage your child to add his or her own prayers to each section.

- ■ **Praise** God for being real to you in church. Be specific.

- ■ **Ask** God to teach your child the kinds of attitudes and actions that please Him.

- ■ **Confess** and ask forgiveness for a time at church when honoring self was more important than honoring God.

- ■ **Thank** God for being in the church worship so that you both could see Him.

If you have any questions, please feel free to discuss them with any of the leaders in the children's ministry program.

Bible Memory Verse

God placed all things under [Jesus'] feet and appointed [Jesus] to be head over everything for the church (Ephesians 1:22).

Note: Early elementary verse in bold type.

God is so spectacular! You've found clue six in your search for God. This week we ducked out of the way of the Geyser of Greatness. We can do this by being humble and keeping our thoughts on God at church.

What's a geyser? It's hot water and steam that pushes up out of the ground and whooshes into the air like a fountain. So when we see the Geyser of Greatness gushing toward us, we need to DUCK!

Color and cut out clue 6. Cut several 4-inch pieces of curling ribbon. Curl them halfway, and glue the straight ends streaming off the worshipers like sun beams. Then glue the clue over #6 on your treasure map.

We find God at Church.

Dear Parents and Guardians,

Please check off the items your child completed this week:

- ❑ Prayer Challenge
- ❑ Map Clue
- ❑ Memory Verse

Adult Signature: _____

FAST TRACK! TICKET

On the Fast Track!

Dear Parents:

Today our children learned from Luke 10:30–37 that <u>we can find God working anywhere and everywhere</u>. God's followers respond to His presence by helping and caring for others. Talk with your child about a time God used you to help someone else or when God used someone else to help you. Prompt your child to remember a time someone helped him or her. Close this time in prayer using the guide below and encouraging your child to add his or her own prayers to each section.

Prayer Challenge

- **Praise** God for how He uses His followers to help others.
- **Ask** God to help you both to act in love and kindness toward others.
- **Confess** and ask forgiveness for a time when your child didn't help someone in need.
- **Thank** God for a kindness someone showed recently, and that people in other places can find God, too.

As you pray together every week, your child will become more comfortable praying out loud. If you have any questions, we encourage you to discuss them with children's ministry leaders.

Bible Memory Verse

The King will reply, "I tell you the truth, **whatever you did for one of the least of these brothers of mine, you did for me**" (Matthew 25:40).

Note: Early elementary verse in bold type.

Is God great or what? He can do anything! You've found clue 7 in your search for God. This week we figured out how to keep away from the stink of the Trash Heap of Heartlessness.

People matter to God. So He is pleased when we care for others. God is working in the world all the time. Often He uses people to help each other, and God can use you, too! When we care for someone, we stay clear of the Stink of the Trash Heap of Heartlessness.

Color and cut out clue 7. In the middle, draw a picture showing how you can care for someone in your family, in your neighborhood, or in your church. Then glue it over #7 on your treasure map.

Don't forget to complete your clues and bring your map to class on _____ to win a prize!

We can find God anywhere and everywhere.

Dear Parents and Guardians,

Please check off the items your child completed this week:

- ☐ Prayer Challenge
- ☐ Map Clue
- ☐ Memory Verse

Adult Signature: _____

FAST TRACK! TICKET

On the Fast Track!

Dear Parents:

Today, our children learned from 1 Kings 19:1–18 that <u>we find God in times when we're afraid</u>. Talk with your child about the kinds of things that cause you both to be afraid. Read the Bible passage and see what scared Elijah and what he did about it. How will your child find God when faced with a fearful experience? Conclude by praying together, using the guide below. Encourage your child to add his or her own prayers to each section.

Prayer Challenge

- **Praise** God for always being with you, even when you're afraid.
- **Ask** God to show you He's with you the next time you're afraid.
- **Confess** the last time you let fear get hold of you instead of trusting in God's help and presence.
- **Thank** God that He will show Himself to you when you look for Him.

If you have any questions, please feel free to discuss them with the children's ministry program leaders.

Bible Memory Verse

I will trust and not be afraid. The LORD, the LORD is my strength and my song (Isaiah 12:2).

Good job! You found the eighth clue in your search for God. This week we didn't want to sink into the Bog of Fear. A bog is a place where the ground is always wet like a squishy sponge. Lots of bugs live there, along with birds and frogs. Instead of falling into the Bog of Fear, we learned how to leap over it by calling out for God and looking for Him when we're scared.

Color and cut out clue 8. Today you'll make a Bog Bug to remind you to look for God when you are afraid. Use things you can find around the house to make a bug: egg carton cup, marshmallows, cereal, toothpicks, macaroni, etc. Tape your Bog Bug to clue 8, then glue it over #8 on your map.

We find God in times when we're afraid.

Dear Parents and Guardians,

Please check off the items your child completed this week:

- ☐ Prayer Challenge
- ☐ Map Clue
- ☐ Memory Verse

Adult Signature: _____

FAST TRACK! TICKET

On the Fast Track!

Dear Parents:

Today our children learned that <u>God is there in the middle of our excitement</u>. Our Bible passages were Psalm 150 and 2 Samuel 22. This week, to reinforce this concept, talk with your child about a really exciting time in your life. Discuss a memory of an exciting time in your child's life too. You could write the memory down or have your child illustrate it and post it on the refrigerator so your child can praise God every time he or she sees the picture. Finish by praying together using the guide below and encouraging your child to add his or her own prayers to each section.

Prayer Challenge

- **Praise** God for being the Creator of all good things who is present in your times of excitement.
- **Ask** God to remind you to give Him the place of honor when life gets exciting.
- **Confess** any times you've forgotten about God when life gets exciting.
- **Thank** God that He makes your life so interesting and fun.

Encourage your child as he or she becomes more comfortable praying out loud. If you have any questions about this lesson, please discuss them with those of us in the children's ministry program.

Bible Memory Verse

The LORD lives! Praise be to my Rock! Exalted be God, the Rock, my Savior! (2 Samuel 22:47).

Awesome! You discovered the ninth clue in your search for God. This week we figured out how to step into the Footholds of Remembrance. What's a foothold? It's a safe place to put your feet when you're climbing up a steep rock. When we give honor to God in our exciting times, it's like finding the right places to put our feet as we travel toward the treasure.

Color and cut out clue 9. Show how special God is by coloring His name with glitter or glitter glue. Then glue the clue over #9 on your treasure map.

We find God in the middle of excitement.

GOD

Dear Parents and Guardians,

Please check off the items your child completed this week:

- ❏ Prayer Challenge
- ❏ Map Clue
- ❏ Memory Verse

Adult Signature: _____

FAST TRACK! TICKET

On the Fast Track!

Dear Parents:

Today our children learned from the Book of Job that <u>God is there with us even when we are sick</u>. To reinforce the concept, talk with your children about what it feels like to be sick and why it's easy to forget about God then. Make a note of encouragement for a friend or family member who's not feeling well. Close this time by praying together using the guide below. Encourage your child to add his or her own prayers to each section.

■ *Praise* God for being in control of all our circumstances.

■ *Ask* God for healing, comfort, and encouragement for sick friends or family.

■ *Confess* anything you've done or said that would make God unhappy or displeased.

■ *Thank* God for any recently answered prayer.

Thank your child for spending time with you in prayer. As always, if you have any questions, please discuss them with leaders in the children's ministry program.

Prayer Challenge

Bible Memory Verse

On my bed I remember you; I think of you through the watches of the night. **Because you are my help, I sing in the shadow of your wings** (Psalm 63:6–7).

Note: Early elementary verse in bold type.

Way to go! You found clue ten in your search for God. This week we talked about getting out of the Muck of Misery. It isn't fun to be sick. But if we remember to look for God when we're sick, His healing and comfort are there for us. We won't get *stuck in the muck*!

Color and cut out clue 10. Then, find small, round objects that look like "pills" to glue in the border of your clue: beads, cereal, beans, buttons. This clue will remind you that God is with you when you are sick. Healing and comfort come from Him. Attach the clue over #10 on your treasure map.

Don't forget to bring your completed treasure map back to class on _____ for a reward!

God is there... even when we are sick.

Dear Parents and Guardians,

Please check off the items your child completed this week:

❑ Prayer Challenge
❑ Map Clue
❑ Memory Verse

Adult Signature: _____

FAST TRACK! TICKET

On the Fast Track!

Dear Parents:

Today our children learned from 1 Kings 17:7–24 that <u>God is with us when we are sad</u>. Talk with him or her about specific ways your family can cope when sad things happen. Perhaps consider the example of someone you both know who's going through a sad time. Pray about what God might want you to do for that person. Finish with prayer together:

- **Praise** God for knowing what is

Prayer Challenge

going on at all times in your lives.

- **Ask** to see God's help or presence when you're experiencing a sadness.
- **Confess** any wrongs recently committed.
- **Thank** God for always being there to comfort you.

As you pray together every week, your child will become more comfortable praying out loud. If you have any questions, please discuss them with those of us involved in running this program.

Bible Memory Verse

Why are you downcast, O my soul? Why so disturbed within me? Put your hope in God (Psalm 42:5).

You're doing great! You found clue 11 in your search for God. This week we talked about walking through the Valley of Sorrow. A valley is a low, flat place between mountains. Sometimes when we're sad, it feels like we're alone in a valley with mountains all around us. But two things we know for sure: God is there with us, and we can talk to Him when we are sad. Knowing that will turn your Valley of Sorrow into a Valley of Peace.

Color and cut out clue 11 to make a peaceful valley. Cut two "cups" from an egg carton. Glue one cup on each side of the river. Glue the clue over #11 on your treasure map. Remember that you can talk to God in sad times. He is with you!

God is with us when we are sad.

Dear Parents and Guardians,

Please check off the items your child completed this week:

- ☐ Prayer Challenge
- ☐ Map Clue
- ☐ Memory Verse

Adult Signature: _____

FAST TRACK! TICKET

On the Fast Track!

Prayer Challenge

Dear Parents:

Today your child learned from 1 Samuel 1 that <u>we can find God even when things seem unfair</u>. Ask your child about a time when things were unfair and how he or she handled it. What could he or she have done differently? Together brainstorm ideas that will help your child handle future situations. Finish your time together with prayer and encourage your child to personalize each section.

- **Praise** God for being in charge and having a perfect plan for your lives.
- **Ask** God to increase your trust in Him when things are unfair, and show how He's there in the unfair times.
- **Confess** and accept God's forgiveness for grumbling instead of trusting God's plan.
- **Thank** God for a recent situation when you found God in your lives. Thank God, too, that your child is becoming more comfortable praying with you every week.

Important!: Please remind your child to bring the treasure map to class next week.

Bible Memory Verse

We live by faith, not by sight (2 Corinthians 5:7).

You're almost there! You found clue 12 in your journey toward the treasure. This week we talked about the Thorns of Unfairness. When something feels unfair, it's like being pricked by a thorn. It hurts to be pricked by a thorn, doesn't it? When life seems unfair, we have to trust God and know that His plan for us is a good one. This will keep us from being pricked by the Thorns of Unfairness.

Color and cut out clue 12. Make it better by adding toothpick "thorns" with glue. Then glue the clue over #12 on your treasure map. This clue will remind you that God knows what's going on in our lives!

Don't forget to bring your map to class next week to get a reward!

We can find God even when things seem unfair.

Dear Parents and Guardians,

Please check off the items your child completed this week:

- ☐ Prayer Challenge
- ☐ Map Clue
- ☐ Memory Verse

Adult Signature: _____

FAST TRACK! TICKET

On the Fast Track!

Dear Parents:

Today our children learned from Luke 15:3–10 that <u>God constantly searches for us</u>. You could reinforce the truth that God searches for us by telling your child how God found you—your salvation testimony—and how you accepted Him as your Lord and Savior. Talk together about your child's decision to follow Christ. If your child hasn't chosen to follow Jesus yet, ask if he or she wants to. Then guide your child in prayer.

Prayer Challenge

Close this time together with the suggested prayer ideas below, allowing your child to personalize the sections:

- **Praise** God for having such a huge love for you that He keeps searching for you until you come to Him.
- **Ask** Jesus to become your Savior, or pray that another person will choose to follow Jesus.
- **Confess** any sin that hasn't been taken to God yet, and receive His forgiveness.
- **Thank** God for loving us so much He keeps searching for us.

Bible Memory Verse

Oh LORD, you have searched me and you know me (Psalm 139:1).

Congratulations!

You found the treasure: *God constantly searches for us!* Look at the treasure map to the right. Trace the path with your finger from the Mountains of Forgetfulness to the Treasure. See if you can name the Bible Truth you learned for each place on the map.

When you get to the Treasure, remember that GOD CONSTANTLY SEARCHES FOR US! He will never lose or forsake us.

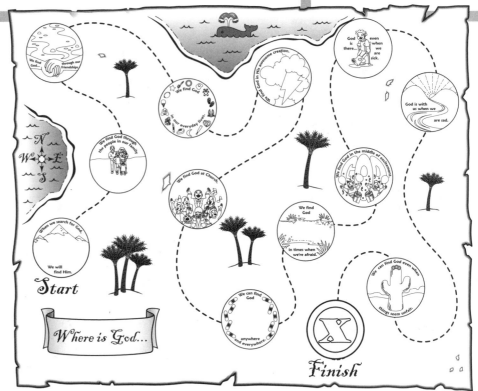

Dear Parents and Guardians,

Please check off the items your child completed this week:

- ☐ Prayer Challenge
- ☐ Map Clue
- ☐ Memory Verse

Adult Signature: _____

FAST TRACK! TICKET